ENDING THE QUEST FOR SOMETHING MORE

Jay E. Adams

Institute for Nouthetic Studies, a ministry of Mid-America Baptist Theological Seminary, 2095 Appling Road, Memphis, TN 38016
mabts.edu / nouthetic.org / INSBookstore.com

Ending the Quest for Something More
by Jay E. Adams
Copyright © 2020 by the Institute for Nouthetic Studies.

New Testament quotations are from the *Christian Counselor's New Testament and Proverbs*
Copyright © 2019 by the Institute for Nouthetic Studies,
© 1977, 1980, 1994, 2000 by Jay E. Adams
Old Testament quotations are from the New American Standard Version

ISBN: 978-1-949737-09-7 (Print)
ISBN: 978-1-949737-10-3 (eBook)
Editor: Donn R. Arms
Design: James Wendorf | www.FaithfulLifePublishers.com

Library of Congress Cataloging-in-Publication Data
Names: Adams, Jay E., 1929-
Title: Ending the Quest for Something More / Jay E. Adams
Description: Memphis: Institute for Nouthetic Studies, 2019
Identifiers: ISBN 978-1-949737-09-7 (paper)
Classification: DDC 248.2

All rights reserved. No part of this publication may be reproduced, stored in a retrieval system, or transmitted in any form or by any means – electronic, mechanical, photocopy, recording, or any other – except for brief quotations in printed reviews, without prior permission of the publisher.

Published in the United States of America

25 24 23 22 21 20   1 2 3 4 5

Preface

This book was written for Christians. If you do not believe in Jesus Christ as your Savior, I want to say just a word to you as well. Many who think they are Christians are not. They have the mistaken idea that if they are not Jews or Muslims, they are Christians. But God says:

> He came to His own creation, and His own people didn't receive Him. But to as many as did receive Him, He gave the right to become God's children; to those who believe in His Name (John 1:11, 12).

These verses make it clear that a Christian is one who "receives" Jesus Christ in order to become God's child. That is the basic question – have you received Jesus or not?

— "Well, what does receiving Jesus mean?" you ask.

Let me explain. Jesus came into the world as the promised Messiah. But when He came in fulfillment of the many biblical prophecies, some did not want to "receive" (welcome) Him for the One that He is. To those who *did* "receive" Him, God granted the right to call themselves His children.

— "But how does one receive, or welcome, Jesus?"

God gave people the right to call themselves His children if they believe in His Name. So, it is by faith in Jesus that a person is admitted into God's family when he believes that Jesus is the One that His name indicates He is.

Now, the name "Jesus" was not, like our names, picked out because His mother Mary liked the sound of it. Rather, it was a name that an angel told her to call Him: "…you must name Him Jesus, because He will save His people from their sins" (Matthew 1:21). "Jesus," in English means "Savior." Here, we see that Jesus is named according to what He came to do – to save those who would believe in Him as the Savior.

— "What is a 'Savior?'"

Apart from what He did, a person will die and have to face God with his sins unforgiven. But Jesus came to "save" (rescue) His own from God's punishment for their sins. God says, "all have sinned and come short of the glory of God" (Romans 3:23). There will be no sin in heaven. No one will go to heaven unless forgiven. Instead, he will be eternally punished for those sins in hell.

— "But what did Jesus do? How does He save?"

Jesus came to die on the cross in the place of guilty sinners, taking the punishment for them. He saves from hell those who receive Him as the One Who took their place. If they confess that they are sinners who need a Savior and believe that He is theirs, then – and only then – will they become God's children.

To fulfill your quest, trust Jesus Christ as the living, resurrected Lord Who died in the place of guilty sinners like you. If you do so, then read the rest of this book, but not before doing so. If you have trusted Jesus after reading this preface, please contact the publisher, so they may send you some further information.

— Jay Adams

Table of Contents

Introduction 7
1. What Do The Scriptures Say? 12
2. False Directions 16
3. Potential for Change 24
4. Regeneration 28
5. The Abundant Life – What Is It? 33
6. Claims by Christians 38
7. But Wait a Moment! 46
8. What Shall We Say? 52
9. Basic Biblical Considerations 55
10. Dimming the Glare 59
11. Solar Eclipse? 64
12. Who's Right? 71
13. The Path of the Righteous 73
14. Growth Is the Right Metaphor 80
15. Renewal of the Image 87
16. The Spiritual Life 92
17. So, How About It? 98

Introduction

Seeking Something More

There is a yearning in the human heart that is hard to satisfy. It is a yearning for "something more." People hunger for a deeper understanding and meaning of life. They long for something that will relieve the deep unease that haunts them in their more reflective moods. Unbelievers vainly try to find this "something" in man and his works, or in the creation. But because they end up worshipping the creature rather than the Creator, they find that these false gods let them down.

Ever since Augustine, Christians have spoken of "a void that only God can fill." For quite some time that sentiment seems to have stood many in good stead. But no longer does it satisfy the insatiable appetite of modern believers. To them, Augustine's words seem hollow, lacking depth and devoid of the explicit direction that they want. There is a hunger for something more (hereafter referred to as SM). And because they fail to find SM, many Christians have joined the world's lament singing its mournful melody and bitter lyrics. Why is this so? That's the question.

Believers Too?

We might expect non-Christians to express dissatisfaction with life – but believers? Yes, believers! They too have joined the melancholy crowd, perhaps voicing the loudest demands. They insist that God enable them to live the "abundant life" that they seem so far from attaining. Deep down inside, many wonder if Christianity is all that it is cracked up to be. "If I have been regenerated, why am I not living life on a higher plane—as Ruth Paxton claimed I can?" That sort of nagging question plagues many earnest Christians.

Have you harbored such thoughts? Perhaps you have said as much to your pastor, a friend or a Christian counselor. Possibly you brood over the lack silently. Conceivably, you have cried out to God for a life of greater fruitfulness. Well, if you are experiencing Augustine's "void," then you should recognize that you are not alone.

Throughout history, the church has had to face the fact that many of its members seek SM. But the tragedy is this quest has led them into all sorts of wrong paths. They have followed formulas that let them down, agonized in prayer that made no discernible difference, walked aisles innumerable times, or defected to cults that only led to dead ends. Some have been so desperate that they have given up, allowing the persistent problem to all but destroy their Christian walk. The apostle John faced the problem in his pastoral ministry to Christians. On one occasion, he found it necessary to write,

> Watch yourselves, that you don't lose that which you have worked for, but rather that you may receive a full reward. Everyone who goes beyond, and doesn't remain in the teaching of Christ, doesn't have God (II John 8, 9).

Already, in New Testament times, Christians were being lured away from the truth by siren voices that promised something "beyond" what John taught them. They too were looking for SM. And you may be sure that there has always been (and always will be) a host of seductive voices assuring them that "We can give you what you seek." That is the great danger. Once a person sets out on a quest for SM he opens himself to every spiritual snake oil salesman in sight.

The Selfish "Solution"

It wasn't long after the apostles died that men, seeking SM, left other Christians to hole up in the caves of North Africa. But these recluses failed to find what they sought. That is because, like all who do such things, they were self-centered. Proverbs 18:1 says, "He who separates himself from others seeks to satisfy his own desire; he rolls headlong against all sound wisdom." They wanted to obey the first great commandment (to love God), but failed to heed the second (to love your neighbor) – from whom they selfishly withdrew. We must never divorce the two commands. To abandon one is to abandon both. Indeed, Paul inseparably combined the two commandments into one when he wrote, "The entire law is summed up in this one statement, 'Love your neighbor as yourself.'" (Galatians 5:14). Loving your neighbor *begins* with loving your closest one – God – Who by the Spirit dwells within you!

But this asceticism doesn't end there. Mysticism of every sort eventually leads to elitism: "I have achieved union with God," the mystic claims. When asked to explain his experience he demurs: "But it was so transcendently glorious that it is inexpressible." So he says. When he found the greater "experience" that he sought, what happens to other persons became inconsequential. But, alas, the "experience" did not last. In no time it faded, leaving the mystic himself with a yearning for more of the same.

Now, the monastic movement that grew out of this asceticism, in time, led to the agonies of Martin Luther. He found that it failed to satisfy. Try as he did, he could not discover the SM that he sought in the solitary life. This was a common experience of the monks. In his *Introduction to A Devout Life*, Francis De Sales put his finger on the problem:

Uneasiness proceeds from an inordinate desire of being delivered from the evil which we feel, or of acquiring the good which we desire. Yet there is nothing more which tends to increase evil and to prevent the enjoyment of good than an uneasy mind.

This "uneasy mind" is the natural fruit of asceticism. Paul pegged it in Colossians 2:23: "...their supposed humility and ascetic treatment of the body...are of no value in keeping the flesh from satisfying itself." "Satisfying itself!" – that's it! But satisfying self rather than God makes true satisfaction impossible! Asceticism, designed to do the opposite, actually focuses one's thinking upon the flesh. The "good" of which De Sales wrote eludes such persons. Mysticism and asceticism offer nothing lasting, and their results in no way resemble the "abundant life" of Scripture.

Protestant Yearnings

About a hundred years ago, in words that put the matter starkly, A.T. Pierson wrote, "The greatest demand of our day is for a higher type of piety on the part of God's children." That's it! That is what so many Christians seek, but so few find. Why don't they? What's wrong? Well, it's impossible to find the pot of gold at the end of the rainbow when you can never locate its beginning. So the troubling question remains, "How can the quest be *rightly* ended?"

Not long after Pierson uttered his lament, Illingworth said, "All our instincts and aspirations are for [a] larger, richer, fuller life." And Alexander MacClaren sighed, "How much more of God we might have! We draw on but a tiny cup full from that great ocean...We live...on the fringe of the land." R. A. Webb noted, "Christian experience is always dissatisfied with itself – the deeper the experience the deeper the discontent. Every child of God aches to be better." Is that how it should be? More recently, in her book, *Jaded*, editor A.J. Kiesling put it baldly, "The only problem with this formula for abundant living is that it doesn't work." She went on to say, "No wonder a tired flock of sheep has wandered back into the barnyard hungry, bleating, pathetic…" Why is this? What is the cause of such abject failure? Is it God's fault? Has He promised much but delivered little? Are the Spirit's resources so meager that it is impossible for Him to help us live joyfully and fruitfully? Why are so many Christians making the trek in search of SM?

Today, as we see, concern is strongly voiced. It is out in the open. Stafford declared, "…any Christian's relationship with God is largely unfulfilled potential." He continued, "Underlying everything…is a great sneaking disappointment: the discrepancy between what he was offered…and what he actually experiences." Does that strike a chord? Does Stafford's thrust probe a sore spot? If so, clearly something is wrong – what is it?

The problem that haunts thinking Christians who wish to obey their Lord, is what this book is all about. There are Christians defeated, discouraged, and downcast because they just can't discover the route to a fuller Christian experience. In it, I intend to call them – indeed, you – to consider the matter. The fundamental question that I want to pose is this: "Is there really a need for SM?" Are seekers right in longing for it? If so, then we must discover how to obtain it. If not, then we must grapple once and for all with the nearly universal desire for it, and the almost universal failure to attain it. In other words, the goal of this volume – in one way or another – is to bring the quest for SM to an *end*. I think, if you pay close attention, follow the argument to its conclusion, you can do so to your satisfaction.

1

What Do The Scriptures Say?

There is no doubt about the existence of a fundamental dissatisfaction among many Christians. Let's take that as a "given." But what's behind it? Clearly, the source is twofold. On the one hand, life without prevailing feelings of joy and peace is miserable. To slog one's way along day after day is a major factor in the yearning for SM: "There *must* be something better than this!" But that isn't all. Indeed, it isn't even the most important factor. The truth is that the Bible itself contributes to the longing we have been describing by telling the reader about the coming of "abundant" living (John 10:10). When we do not live as we believe God wants us, that too produces confusion and guilt which, in turn, leads to more bad feelings. Then, the question becomes, "What am I doing wrong?"

What *is* Wrong?

Confusion, yes. But is the guilt justified? From the New Testament description of the Christian life, it would seem so. Consider the following: If the kingdom of God is not a matter of "eating and drinking, but righteousness and peace and joy by the Holy Spirit" (Romans 14:17) then why don't we experience more joy and peace? And why is there so much unrighteousness among Christians? If, as Jesus said, "I came so that they may have life – in abundance," why don't His "bleating" sheep live this abundant life (a consideration that may in time lead one to ask, "Am I really one of the sheep?")?

On the other hand, one may wonder whether the scriptural description of the new life has been overstated. Another wonders, "Is there something wrong with the faith itself?" Or is there a common failure to correctly interpret such passages as those just mentioned, so that we have read more into them than we should have? What is the answer to such questions?

Plainly, pleasing passages like those cited above encourage the believer to expect SM than what he has, don't they? If so, then why aren't we able to realize such high expectations? Listen to this: "Now may the God of hope fill you with every sort of joy and peace in believing, so that you may have an abundance of hope by the Holy Spirit" (Romans 15:13). That was a benediction prayer. Was Paul's prayer answered? Did the Romans actually receive this *abundant* hope? Did they experience "every sort of joy and peace" through "believing?" If so, shouldn't believers today also expect similar blessings? Why don't Christians generally exhibit "every sort of" joy and peace? And, what about "abundance of hope?" Aren't there many discouraged believers who have lost hope? Certainly, Paul seems to have in mind an experience that transcends that which most Christians know anything about. Or does he? Or – do others have it, and it's just you and I who don't?

Biblical Encouragement to Seek SM

Without question, Paul calls for SM when addressing the Thessalonian church. He mentions the "faith and love" that the members of that church already exhibited (I Thessalonians 3:6), but then goes on to say, "May the Lord make your love for one another and for all people increase and abound just as ours does for you." "Increase and abound!" There it is again – that abounding nature of the Christian experience. And "increase." He isn't satisfied with mere faith and love – he wants *more*! SM! Indeed, he goes on to say, "you yourselves have been taught by God how to love one another...But we urge you, brothers, that you continue to do so even more and more" (I Thessalonians 4:9, 10). God taught them, he says. But did God fail to teach them to love to the degree that Paul expected? Just how much more did he expect? *Perfect* love – or something less? Does he call for more than God provides? Or, more of it? All of this is perplexing to the average Christian. In many churches today, if faith, hope, and love were present among the brothers to *any* noticeable extent, we would be so happy to see it so that we would think that we had almost "arrived." But Paul wants "more" – and still "more." Is it possible? And is it right to hold out such high standards as goals if it isn't possible to attain to them? Or, on the other hand, is there a way to do so?

Certainly, if the Scriptures tell us anything about the Christian life, we have seen that they say it ought to be peaceful and joy-filled and that it ought to be possible for us to become righteous enough to "please" God in what we do. And if it is true that God "is producing in [us] both the willingness and the ability to do the things that please Him" as Paul told the Philippians (Philippians 2:13), then why is it that we don't please Him as we should? Will He really "produce" in every Christian the willingness and the ability that He promises? Are these boons only for the few and not for you and me? Or is there a secret in obtaining them that we don't know? Why do we live at so low a level? Or, is it all that low? Where is Ruth Paxton's "life on a higher plane?" Does it exist? Should we expect it? Is it proper to hold out the prospect of living it?

True, the Scriptures tell us much about our sinfulness. They exhort, rebuke, and warn. There is no hiding the fact, as Paul tells us in Romans 7, that he too struggled to do what he wanted to do only to find himself doing what he didn't want to do. That description more nearly matches our situation, doesn't it? But then, again, Peter tells his readers, "You haven't seen Him, but you love Him…and you rejoice with inexpressible and glorious delight" (I Peter 1:8). How can there be such "delight" during this struggle? Were the early Christians of an entirely different breed? Were they able to do what most of us cannot? Are you *filled* with *inexpressible joy?* Does your faith bring you *glorious delight?* Well, perhaps it does for you. You may be the exception to the rule. But, if you can take the writings of mature Christians for a fact, they will tell you they don't know much of this sort of thing.

A Perplexing Problem

Well, we leave the biblical references that we have noted (we could have filled pages with similar ones), thoroughly perplexed. We are called to extraordinary living, promised marvelous things, and read the prayers of the apostles for others that, presumably, they expected to enter into abundant living. Were the apostles' prayers answered? Were they answered minimally rather than maximally? Do we interpret such passages properly or improperly? Shear honesty compels us to ask, "What is the answer to these sticky and troublesome questions?"

The book that you are reading does not avoid the issues. It doesn't cover up the inner yearnings and bewilderment that gnaw at the very guts of so many believers. Instead, it faces these matters in a thoughtful, serious, and biblical manner. In it, you may not find complete answers to every question that you ask, but you should find many. Indeed, I would not want to hold before you the hope of absolute finality in these matters since it is precisely such hope that I wish to dispel.

2

False Directions

When traveling to a vaguely known destination without a road map, a person is largely directionless. Usually, after wandering about for a time, he will stop and ask directions of those he meets. Some are quite willing to accommodate him – whether or not they really know how to get to the place he tries to describe. As a result, he may find himself chasing all over the place, ending up more confused than when he began.

Many who willingly guide the earnest seeker on his quest for SM claim to have been there themselves. They will tell him how to locate the rainbow and describe the contents of the pot of gold that he will find at its end. Such illusory hopes that they raise may energize and buoy up the seeker for a time, but after he has chased the ever-eluding rainbow for a while in vain, if he doesn't give up on his quest altogether, he may turn to someone else for directions. Eventually, the seeker after SM may deceive himself, thinking at last he has found what he is seeking, if a persuasive guide is able to assure him that his version of the abundant life is the correct one.

False directions from spiritually blind guides who dare to lead the blind, in the end bring bitter despair to the genuine seeker who demands fine gold in that pot, and will accept nothing less. Others may take longer to discover that "all that glitters isn't gold." But sooner or later, the one who learns that he has been led astray – if not embittered – becomes even more confused than he was before setting out on his quest. At length, he may give up in despair. So, in order to warn seekers of the danger of accepting false guidance, let's consider a few of these false guides and the misleading directions that they offer.

Pantheistic Mysticism

I have already mentioned mysticism in the previous chapter so I will say little about it here. Because it points one in some direction other than to biblical revelation and the Savior of whom that revelation speaks, mysticism is seriously flawed. Instead of some road to SM that God revealed, mysticism assures the seeker that he can have an immediate union with God. Thus, the mystic way leads *away* from the rainbow rather than toward it. Mysticism, with its proud, selfish, elitist claim to have achieved union with the divine, should be especially abhorrent to thinking Christians. That is so not only because of how this form of pantheism dishonors God, and what it does to the self-deceived seeker, but also because of how it estranges him from others.

You can readily see these traits of mysticism in the writings of Bernard:

> This commingling of the Word [here he refers to Jesus Christ] with the soul is purely spiritual…The rapture of the pure soul to God, and God's most blest descent into the soul, these constitute a union which takes place in the spirit…A soul in this condition, so loving and so loved, will not be satisfied with the sort of manifestation through created things that is given to everyone, nor even with the dreams and visions granted to the few. It will demand a special privilege – not an appearance but an inward inpouring.

Note the dissatisfaction with anything else but the mystical experience which doesn't last, the elitism (he has been exalted even beyond the "few" who are given dreams and visions!) and a "demand" for nothing less than the "special privilege" of the "union" that supposedly takes place with God. Such unmitigated gall!

We have already noted the warning in Proverbs about separating one's self (Proverbs 18:1). Because of the esoteric nature of this false direction, most Christians will see through it and turn from those who say that mysticism is the way to abundant living.

Asceticism

Much the same may be said of teachers and churches that suggest that the road to SM leads directly to the monastery. The ascetic path, which is akin to mysticism, is more frequently traveled than the pure mystic path. Whole communities of Roman Catholics, Greek, and other Orthodox churches seek SM through becoming a part of these groups, hoping that by disciplines of rejection and self-denial they can find satisfaction. But, as I mentioned, Martin Luther – one of the most sincere practitioners of the ascetic life – exposed the hollowness and utter futility of this "SM." Rather than life on a higher plane, asceticism leads to agonies of soul and, ultimately, to despair. Again, because asceticism is a man-made solution to the problem the seeker desires to solve (remember Colossians 2:23), it cannot bring happiness to those who seek the life of peace and joy.

Perfectionism

Coming closer to home, we should mention those within Protestantism who teach the possibility of sinless perfection. Surely, were one able to achieve such perfection, that would bring boundless joy and peace – an incontrovertible fact that no right-thinking person could deny. However, those hapless advocates of this dismal doctrine can only lead the seeker into the deepest valleys of disillusionment.

According to perfectionists, it is possible to attain to sinlessness in this life. But the obvious fact is that those who teach sinless perfection fail to live sinless lives. They fail the simple biblical test, "by their fruits shall you know them," when it is applied to them by those who monitor their lifestyles. The results of this test quickly disclose the fact that the doctrine is pure deception. Because those who practice the path to perfection never truly achieve it, many live a hypocritical life in which they claim what they themselves know to be false. If some well-meaning, but self-deluded perfectionists are not aware of this deception, it is only because they have set the bar of perfection so low that they can easily vault it. What the Bible recognizes as sins they either gloss over or rename "mistakes, immaturity" or something else.

Again, like the mystic and the ascetic, the perfectionist fails to turn to the Scriptures for the source of his beliefs. He may claim to do so, and by adopting erroneous interpretations of Scripture may even attempt to support it, but he conveniently avoids clear biblical statements that contradict his teaching. And careful exegesis of the passages that he supposes support his teaching prove otherwise. Rather than labor the point, simply listen to this explicit statement of the apostle John: "If we say that we don't have any sin, we deceive ourselves and the truth is not in us" (I John 1:8). This clear denial of the perfectionist position – curiously enough – is found in the very book to which perfectionists do appeal when they speak of having attained to "perfect love."

Flawed exegesis leads perfectionists to believe that passages in I John back their position. They triumphantly appeal to I John 4:12–18. In those verses, John does speak of "perfect love." The translation of the word "perfect," however, might more accurately be translated "complete." What it indicates is that someone or something has completed, or *accomplished,* some purpose. However, the love referred to is God's love toward us; not ours toward Him. When God completes his work of love in us, for instance, we no longer need fear. John does not teach that a believer can attain to perfection of love in this life. If he had said so, he would have contradicted himself: see once again I John 1:8 (also v. 10). The passages perfectionists rely on merely teach that when God's love is "perfected" it "has achieved its purposes." The verses in I John 4 have to do with growth, sanctification, and the process of becoming more like Christ; not with some sort of pre-death glorification! Listen to the passages in question (translated more closely) and you will see what John had in mind:

> Nobody has ever seen God, but if we love one another, God remains in us and His love accomplishes its purpose in us (4:12).
>
> For this has love accomplished its purpose in us, that we may have boldness on the Judgment Day (4:17).
>
> ...love that has accomplished its purpose throws fear out... (4:18).

In these verses, we see what happens in a believer when God "perfectly" (completely) does something for him. The perfection is in God's operation in the believer; it is not in the latter's attainments.

Second Blessing Movements

Next, think a bit about Pentecostalism and the charismatic movement. Here, we encounter such a wide variety of concepts that it will only be possible to address those views that seem to be most common. Most stress the miraculous gifts of the Spirit (in particular, speaking in tongues) as conclusive evidence that one has entered into a "Spirit-filled" life. This life of "SM" is to be sought at a time subsequent to regeneration, commencing at a second blessing by the Holy Spirit. The great problem with this view is that the Bible teaches no such thing. To expect a supposed, instantaneous coming of the Spirit upon a person following his initial coming at regeneration is quite contrary to biblical teaching. But those who postulate the theory point to Pentecost.

First, the only two times when the Spirit fell on believers in such a fashion was at Pentecost and in the house of Cornelius (Acts 2:3, 17; 10:44). On neither occasion was anyone seeking the experience. Moreover, both of these occasions were special: Peter was using the "keys" Jesus gave him (Matthew 16:18) to unlock the door of the church first to the Jews and then to the Gentiles. Thereafter, gifts were always given by the laying on of the apostles' hands (Acts 8:17, 18; 19:6).

Second, as I have shown in my book *Signs and Wonders in the Last Days*, miracles ceased with the completion of the canon. Joel predicted that the miracles he listed (in the prophecy that Peter quoted on the Day of Pentecost) would take place only during the forty-year interim that would stretch from Pentecost to "the great and notable Day of the Lord" (the destruction of Jerusalem in 70 AD). In Acts 2:20 he described this forty-year time period as "before" (or running up to) that Day. There was no expectation that such revelatory gifts would be needed after the entire New Testament had been completed, as it was by that date.

Advocates of charismatic doctrine identify the supposed Spirit-filled life with the abundant life. Many who have been caught up in this movement while seeking SM, in time have found it to be a false way – usually to their utter chagrin. Others, still ensnared in the deception, have learned how to keep themselves lathered up emotionally in an attempt to produce their futile imitation of what the Bible calls "abundant" living.

Quietism

There are, in addition to those groups mentioned above, the quietists. Quietism is the view held by Quakers, Keswick teachers and others. By following several steps (originally four but later five), Keswick teaches that one can be catapulted up into a more ethereal-like sphere that Ruth Paxton called "Life on a Higher Plane." As the crucial step, their SM is supposedly attained by "yielding" one's self to God. Often this act (not a process) of yielding is called "total surrender." Quietists urge Christians to "let go and let God." By this commonly used slogan, they mean that one must stop trying to find SM by his own efforts. Every effort that he makes toward that end is fleshly; God must do it for him, instead of him.

For a succinct presentation of the Keswick process see J. Robertson McQuilkin's, "*The Keswick Perspective.*" An interesting refutation, from the point of view of personal experience with the Keswick view, you may turn to no less a theologian than J. I. Packer. Packer tells of his involvement in the movement as a young Christian, and how after much yielding and surrendering he concluded, "…The expected experience was not coming. The technique was not working."

There are insurmountable problems with the quietist's view. Most of its sincere practitioners find that they must yield over and over again. The joy and peace promised just don't stick! This fact severely blunts the supposed satisfaction that they claim to find at the outset, since it demonstrates that there really is no "victorious life" of sustained joy and peace as was promised. But there is a more obvious objection to quietism: how is it that the Bible is full of commands for the Christian to "do" this or that to attain joy and peace from God? If all that is needed is to let God do what is required *for* us, *instead of* us, then these commands make little sense and only confuse matters. If the quietist's version of sanctification were true, the Bible would be a much thinner volume! And, to clinch matters, consider the fact that to be able to surrender or yield *totally*, one would already have to be totally surrendered or yielded. There is no place for him to say, "I believe; help me with my unbelief" (Mark 9:24).

All of the systems mentioned – as well as others that could be – offer SM. It is, of course, that which gives them their appeal. And because of the laudable and legitimate desire to be more righteous and holy before God, believers are often attracted to them. In addition to the errors mentioned above, sadly, the church has failed to teach biblical facts about living abundantly. Consequently, the desire for SM has caused many to seek it elsewhere. In the chapters that follow, I shall try to rectify that situation. Indeed, it is that issue that called forth this book.

3

Potential for Change

It is not enough to refute erroneous doctrines – as crucial as that irksome task may be. We must also proceed to an examination of the biblical evidence for attaining peace and joy in the present life. Without doubt the Bible holds forth the certainty of "life – in abundance" (John 10:10). The word "abundant" means "in excess." The picture is of something that goes beyond, something that is actually more than is needed. That sounds like a worthy quest, doesn't it?

Well, later in this book we shall have to come to grips with exactly what Jesus meant when He uttered the words in John 10:10. And, to do so, we must undertake a study of the change that has already occurred and the change that is potentially possible for every Christian. Believers who recognize that they are far from attaining to joy and peace need to know what, potentially, they may become.

We can say, without equivocation, that biblical change is unlike worldly change. Since Spencer, much of the world thinks that forward movement is desirable change. Unbelievers look forward to Something More. More of the "good things" that money can buy; more of the improvements that science and medicine can provide; more that the government can dole out. Perhaps, in time, even deathlessness! But their hopes are futile. Material and technological progress continues, it is true, and it brings comfort and ease. But despite that, men find themselves faced with the same old problems – misery, misunderstanding, grief, and war. That is because there is no change in human nature. Indeed, yesterday's problems are only magnified when contrasted with progress in other aspects of life. As a result, man's inventions become but megaphones for his cry to overcome failure, sorrow, sin, trouble, and death.

Potential for Biblical Change

Change of a biblical sort, however, *does* have to do with change in human life. It is fundamentally a change from sin toward righteousness; from what displeases God to what pleases Him. In short, in contrast to the world's concern about outer change in man's milieu, it is within human beings themselves that biblical change occurs. And because that is precisely what unbelievers lack, they will not find peace apart from the One Who gives it.

According to Romans 8:8, "Those who are in the flesh [unregenerate men] cannot please God." Unbelievers are incapable of doing so because they have not experienced that change. Their best motives are inadequate because they do not include God's glory. Therefore, they are still estranged from the promised blessings of the Christian life (Ephesians 2:11, 12). Man has no potential for pleasing God apart from Jesus Christ (I John 2:23). "Life abundantly," – whatever that means – belongs exclusively to God's own. But, as we have seen, they too are crying out for SM. How is that so? In light of the promises of Scripture, they recognize that there is far more available to them than what they have. Does that mean that they should set out on a quest for the "Abundant Life?" They are cognizant of the fact that it was said of the Philippians that "it is God Who is producing...both the willingness and the ability to do the things that please Him" (Philippians 2:13). They realize that such a life of obedience doesn't characterize them; the joy and peace that comes from pleasing God is not their day-by-day experience. Something is wrong and they want to know what it is. They are asking how they may remedy the situation. How can *they* get SM?

Potential

Unbelievers once flocked to the Human Potential Movement which was closely associated with Carl Rogers. But they found it wanting. Though *they* did not understand why it was so flawed, Christians knew that it failed because the change held forth was to be brought about by people who had not themselves been changed! The thoughts, feelings, and actions of unregenerate persons failed to reach the supposed "potential;" that was hyped. The failure of this movement lay, in part, in the fact that it did not recognize differences in human "potential' before the fall, after the fall, after regeneration, and after glorification. When Christians speak of the possibility or "potential" for change, they think only of the last two stages of mentioned. They know of no other God-honoring potential for man. And, when they speak of change, they understand this as the work of the Holy Spirit Who can give spiritual life to those "dead in trespasses and sin," a life which alone produces joy and peace from God.

Biblical Potential

Now, "potential" in Christian thinking cannot be measured by modern testing. If any believers ever reached anything near their potential, divinely speaking, it is those mentioned in Hebrews 11, many of whom utterly failed when measured by humanly-devised standards. Jesus did not choose His disciples because of any "potential" He saw in *them*. Instead, He determined to change them so as to work into them the potential for the tasks for which they were chosen.

It is on the grounds of these fundamental biblical truths that any concept of SM must be built. But what is that SM? We still don't fully understand the references to "abundance, joy, peace," and so forth, which are promised.

Its Meaning for Us

What is "potential" anyway? The word comes from the same stem as "potent" and refers to the power or capacity to do something. Potential, then, is unused capacity, untapped power. In Christian terms, it includes

1. The resources that are inherent in one's nature after regeneration;
2. The power available from the indwelling of that Spirit;
3. The Scriptures "implanted" in the heart of the believer to change his attitudes, his thinking, and his actions;
4. The ministry of the church and the means of Grace.

These resources, which all Christians possess and tap to some extent, provide far greater potential than any Christian in this life even begins to utilize. It is to this issue, then, that we must turn our attention.

4

Regeneration

Unlike sanctification, where the believer plays a part (instigated and assisted by God, to be sure), regeneration is the work of God alone. In order to understand the Christian's potential for SM, which we discussed in part in the previous chapter, you must fully comprehend the biblical facts about regeneration.

The word "regenerate" means "to give birth to again." It is the expression Jesus used when speaking to Nicodemus in John 3:3. It refers, as Jesus affirmed, to being born of the water and the Spirit. John's water baptism represented repentance; Jesus' Spirit baptism was the life-giving work of faith in the person being regenerated. The water was the outer sign of the inner reality. To be born again, then, means to be moved by the Spirit to repent and believe the Gospel.

Terms that Describe Regeneration

Now, several other terms are used in the Scriptures to help us understand the fact, the act, and the effects of this large event. They are also metaphors that portray radical change. Here are the prominent ones:

1. "quickening" or "giving life to" one dead in trespasses and sins (Ephesians 2:1);
2. a "resurrection" in which one is raised from spiritual death to spiritual life (John 5:25);
3. receiving "a new heart" (Ezekiel 36:26);

4. obtaining "freedom from sin's rule" (Romans 6:8; I Peter 1:18), and

5. becoming "a new creation" (II Corinthians 5:17).

What they Indicate

All of these figures point to the immediate, instantaneous act of God that brings about radical change in a human being. Prior to regeneration, a person is alienated from God by sin. Now, by regeneration, the one who was alienated has been brought into a close relationship with Him. But that thought doesn't go far enough to describe what regeneration does. He is so alienated by his sin that he is literally *dead* to God and all things spiritual; he is a child of the devil; he is a ruined creation; his heart is deceitful and so desperately wicked that it is entirely oriented toward sin. He is "in the flesh" and thus cannot please God (Romans 8:8). Indeed, he must be given new life in order to believe and be saved. The giving of that spiritual life is the act that we call "regeneration."

Understanding the concept behind these metaphors is important: they all indicate that the unregenerate person himself is incapable of taking the action needed to make the radical change. A dead person cannot give himself life; a ruined creation needs to be re-created and so on. In addition, they all indicate the need for an external power sufficient to work the mighty change that reverses the alienation from God. And, thirdly, as I said, they indicate that the change takes place in a moment. There is no midground between death and life. One is alive or dead spiritually according to whether he is regenerate or not. There is nothing in these metaphors about a work in process, a period of growth, or a gradual transformation. And, finally, they all indicate actions that belong only to God. He alone is capable of giving life (John 5:26).

Before regeneration, a person is spiritually incapacitated. He cannot please God, and he cannot even welcome, savingly understand, or appropriate the truth of His Word (I Corinthians 2:9-16). This is because he lacks the presence of the Holy Spirit in his life (Romans 8:9). In contrast, regeneration is described as having the Holy Spirit "poured" into the heart (Romans 5:5).

Again, all of the factors involved in the previously mentioned metaphors adhere equally to this one.

One, Not Two Natures

The regenerated person, however, does not receive a "new," additional nature, as some think. The idea of two natures in a believer – one wholly good; the other entirely bad, is foreign and repugnant to Scripture. The believer is one whose old nature is "new" in the sense that it has been changed. It is transformed, "renewed," so as to enable the Christian to know and obey God's Word. This means that he has been given

A new disposition (or orientation): he now can love God and his neighbor;

A new desire (motive): gratitude (II Corinthians 4:1);

A new determination (or commitment): to please God.

The problem expressed by Isaiah is now reversed. Speaking for God, he wrote, "My thoughts are not your thoughts, neither are your ways My ways." (Isaiah 55:8). Being regenerated means that one is now capable of thinking God's thoughts after Him; of travelling the paths of righteousness for His Name's sake, although that does not mean he always will do so. Some things from the past have been carried over into the new life that keep him from fully conforming to God's thoughts and ways.

Spiritual Potential

We have been thinking about "potential." In short, we may say that a regenerate person is the only one who has the potential (power)

- to understand God and His truth;
- to love God and neighbor,
- and to obey God's commandments.

His natural capacities have been reoriented and energized by the Spirit.

As you can see, an individual of this sort has the potential to accomplish much – indeed, much more than he actually does. He is on the path to SM, if anyone is. But does he have the potential to attain to the SM that men seek? Can he find the end of the rainbow and pursue its arch to the end?

Once more, those questions force us to look at the problem we have been considering. We have noted the yearning in the human heart for SM – something more, something better. Believers, as well as unbelievers, seek SM. But the deep yearning of the unbeliever is radically different from that of the believer, and the two must not be equated. Both have a desire for SM, but the believer has abandoned his unbelieving desires for new ones. Consequently, they both have a different idea of what this SM is and, as a result, each looks in a different place for it.

Unbelievers try to find SM in the world, with no reference to God. They are interested only in such things as the environment, human relationships, money, possessions, fame, prestige, power, entertainment, sports – in short, in man and his works. They worship the creature rather than the Creator (Romans 1:25). But, as Ecclesiastes shows so vividly, these things do not satisfy. They are vain ("empty") *because* they do not endure.

Believers, it is true, have a new orientation toward God. They have the spiritual potential to find and enjoy SM. Yet, many are greatly dissatisfied. They are still looking for SM. They go from church to church, read books one after another, attend conferences, yield over and over again, yet never find what they seek. Why? That's the problem. Again, with them, we must ask, "Has Christianity failed?" Or was G.K. Chesterton right when he said, "The Christian ideal has not been tried and found wanting, it has been found difficult; and left untried?" But can that be true? Didn't Paul "try" it? Did he succeed?

Is Jesus not all that He was said to be? Is regeneration all there is? True Christians yearn for the removal of sin, unrighteousness, error, and lust – but like the apostle, struggle with these things (cf. Romans 7:15-23). If one is truly redeemed and – because of the problem we are chasing in this book, some wonder if they are – he may want to know what hinders him from advancing to "abundant" life in Christ. To *shalom*? After all, what does it mean for each man to sit under his vine and fig tree?

The alternatives seem to be

1. Christianity is false (a concept that a Christian simply must not entertain),
2. claims for it have been exaggerated,
3. many have greatly misunderstood the biblical picture of abundant Christian living, or
4. we have largely failed to understand how to access it and realize our potential.

It will be our task (and pleasure) to sort through these options to discover which, if any, of them are true.

5

The Abundant Life – What Is It?

I have frequently referred to the claims Christians make about "The Abundant Life" – a goal to which they aspire. But so far, I have not looked at the passage closely. Jesus' words seem to indicate that He wants us to acquire "something more" than most of us claim to experience—that He is urging us on to a higher form of Christian life. But is that the case? Or have we read into them more than we should have? Have we understood them wrongly? Until now, we have examined John 10:10 only superficially. So, let's more fully examine His words. Jesus said,

> The only reason the thief comes is to kill and destroy; I came so that they may have life – in abundance.

Context

First, note the context. Jesus is describing Himself as the Good Shepherd of the sheep. In verse 10 He contrasts Himself and His purposes with those of the murderous "thieves" who preceded Him (v. 8). They did not care for the flock, only for themselves. They stole into the sheepfold in order to steal, kill, and destroy sheep (v. 1). Who is Jesus describing? He has in mind bad shepherds of God's people throughout the Old Testament era, including many religious and political leaders up to His own time. He sets up a sharp contrast between Himself and these thieves and hirelings. The impact of this contrast is felt especially in Jesus' use of the emphatic word *ego* ("I") in verse 10: They come to steal, kill, and so on, but "*I* came so that they may have life." So, Jesus sets forth His life-giving ministry in stark contrast to the death and destruction that results from bad shepherding.

Life-giving is uppermost in Jesus' mind. What is this "life" like? The life our great Shepherd of the sheep affords is the life about which He often spoke and about which John regularly wrote. Indeed, it is a motif that crops up again and again throughout John's Gospel. The interesting fact is that elsewhere He calls this life "*eternal* life": "Whoever believes in the Son has eternal life…" (John 3:36). And, note, John 6:47: "Let me assure you that whoever believes has eternal life" (John 5:47). In both verses, Jesus makes a striking assertion – this eternal life is a present possession! That is significant.

Abundant Life is "Excessive" Life

In addition, Jesus told His listeners, "Just as the Father has life in Himself, so too He has granted the Son to have life in Himself" (John 8:26). He is the Source and Giver of this life. Pointedly, at His "coming," He brings abundant life to His sheep (v. 10). If the life He gives is eternal life (which commentators believe is qualitative as well as quantitative), then it is not unreasonable to think that he equates *eternal* and *abundant* life. Putting all of this together, is it surprising that when He speaks of the life he has for His sheep, Jesus says that it is "– in abundance" (i.e., literally, in "excess")? And, if that is so – and it seems likely that it is – could not Jesus have been speaking about an important quality of eternal life when He noted that it was excessive? After all, during our earthly life, it is only possible to barely tap the riches and resources of the eternal life we possess. We will be able to appropriate unimaginably more after we have been perfected. But we cannot, and therefore need not, enter into the full abundance of that life in this world. It will take glorified bodies and souls to do so. Then, in our fully redeemed persons, we shall know by experience why Jesus called the treasures of eternal life "excessive" for our present use. We will enjoy that abundant life throughout all eternity in ways that we shall only then be fully capable of doing. So, because we may only in part appreciate and appropriate the true wealth of eternal life at the present time, it must seem excessive to us.

If this understanding of "abundance" (which, remember, means "excess, *more than is needed*") is correct, then Jesus is not promising some sort of abundant life that we ought to strive to live here and now. Indeed, in the passage, He does not exhort; He informs. He is describing, instead, the eternal life that we now possess but can enjoy only minimally. It is the same life that we shall take pleasure in eternally, but present limitations keep us from fully partaking of it.

For Jesus to speak this way of the life He gives, dramatically *emphasizes* the contrast with the murderous thieves who come only to *kill* the sheep. He comes to give *life*! But that is something more than physical life. It is life in "excess" which, in tern, is the same as "eternal" life.

Because this interpretation of "life – in abundance" is correct (and when you read the commentators you will discover that they offer little expository help), you can understand that Jesus was not urging us to seek SM. Instead, the point is that there is always more in this life to be enjoyed, and when one has done so, there is still more – and more and more. We are dealing with something that is always beyond us, because it is of more than sufficient use for this present lifetime.

In John 10:10, then, Jesus is not urging us to strive to enter into "the abundant life," as though it were something that *all* should, but only *some* Christians actually have. The "abundant life" is not SM distinct from the life received in regeneration to be obtained at some time after conversion. Indeed, Jesus was merely *stating the fact* that what He brings is abundant life. He brought it; all genuine believers have it. He brought it for *sheep;* not for *some* sheep). He made no exhortation at all. This life is, therefore, something that we should understand as a present possession of all of true sheep. Jesus makes no distinction between them. In contrast to the thieves and murderers, He brings abundant life to *all* His sheep. To change that in any way is to destroy the wonderful emphasis in the verse.

Limitation Now

As a matter of fact, contrary to exhorting Christians to enter into abundant living, what Jesus taught in John 10:10 is that it is *not possible* to fully enjoy abundant life now. It is life that is over and above what you can expect to enjoy now fully. You will always have SM out in front, toward which you are moving, because it is eternal life. Life in "the kingdom from the heavens" came with Jesus Christ, but it is not distinct from the glorified life we shall come to know after death. Indeed, the two are the same. But a great change will occur at death when we are glorified. The change that takes place, however, is not in the quality or character of the life available, but in us – in our ability to more fully access it. The life we live now is *potentially* the same as what we shall have then. The difference lies in the present limitations and imperfections that prohibit us from entering into it with any sort of completeness. When we are glorified, we shall appreciate in a new and much greater way what we now have.

But, even then, it is possible that we shall still yearn for SM, not in agony or despair as we now sometimes do (longing for relief), but with a desire to go on happily advancing in knowledge and truth to God's glory. Learning will be a joyous movement from truth to greater truth. Not a trek from error to truth (or partial truth) as we now experience. In other words, we will go on experiencing the eternal life we now have, but perfectly. At present, our experience is like trying to absorb an ocean with a paper towel. Who knows how much spiritual treasure shall be able to enjoy in our newly-formed bodies and souls! The only conclusion that we can reach about John 10:10 is that it has been wrongly interpreted. Jesus was not describing "something more" that we might acquire by prayer, conforming to some routine – or whatever. He was describing the new life all believers possess.

In John 10:10 Jesus was declaring that He brought His sheep nothing less than eternal life and, therefore, that they were already in full possession of it. The only exhortation that should be made with reference to the verse, then, is to be sure to recognize what is already yours, and be thankful for and enjoy it to the fullest extent now possible. Clearly, the passage has been sadly misinterpreted. There is no Abundant Life distinct from the life that all believers possess!

Now, because John 10:10 is not the only passage in which the Bible writers seemingly hold out a hope for SM (though surely a principal one), we must investigate others as well. But first, before we do, let's try to understand something about how Christian teachers have described this SM that they tout. The claims coming from various segments of the church are enlightening and true evidence of why it is that believers are in a weary search for the rainbow's gold.

6

Claims by Christians

There are three sorts of claims for SM. There are those made by Christian writers and leaders of all kinds, there are those made directly in the Bible, and there are those that may be inferred from biblical teaching and theological formulations. In this chapter, as promised. I shall consider the first of the three.

Great claims have been made by Christian leaders, inducing many to wonder why they – and other Christians that they know – have failed to attain anything like what these leaders write about. Confusion has arisen from the significant differences among theologians and preachers. Moreover, the writings of these teachers have not always been lucid. Sometimes, the claims are unsupported, at other times reason or Scripture are appealed to. Often, there is mere assertion coupled with some questionable anecdotal "evidence." And, in many cases, no data about how to realize those claims is given. Still, there is much that sounds so persuasive that any serious, thinking Christian must come to grips with it. Let's zero in on some quotations.

Random Quotations

As you peruse these quotations, ask yourself whether or not they are helpful. Try to determine whether they clarify difficult points or whether they further confuse issues. I have not chosen them because they are necessarily incorrect. Nor have I chosen the quotations because they are of crucial significance. Rather, I am concerned to get you to think about the meaning of what you read every day in this area of thought.

- Spiro Zodhaties: "Believers have every reason to be the happiest people on earth." *A Revolutionary Ministry.* Ridgefield: AMG (1974).
    - That affirmation seems, at least on the face of it, to be reasonable. But it is the sort of statement that protrudes from the pages of a book when someone who is far from happy reads it. Should he be exhorted to change and conform to the idea, or is there something wrong with it? Were the apostles so happy that this could be said about them – or, if not, should they have been?

- Illingsworth: "Christianity enables the truest self-development that is possible in this life, and promises its completion hereafter…by overcoming sin in the individual, Christianity liberates the whole personality." *Christian Character.* London: MacMillan (1905), pp. 46, 114.
    - Again, depending on how these words are interpreted, one can see in them a statement about the potential a believer has in Christ through regeneration, the Scriptures and the Holy Spirit. But, then, what about the reference to "the truest self-development?" Is that based upon something that is found in Scripture, or merely an inference from general principles? If the latter, is it right? Should one expect this? And, to what does "hereafter" refer? Eternity, or some point in time before death?

- John Calvin: He says that God gives us "victory against the things that Satan practices to overthrow us…if we call upon Him and put our trust in the strength of His Holy Spirit, it is certain that we shall obtain the victory against all that Satan can ever put in our way." *Sermons on Ephesians*, Edinburgh: The Banner of Truth Trust (1979), p. 518.

- o This is a large and wonderful promise carefully hedged about with a definite qualification. But it leaves the reader to wonder what he means by putting trust "in the strength of the Holy Spirit." Is this a quietistic notion accidentally slipped in by Calvin? Does he mean not to exert effort in the war against the evil one? Surely, John Calvin was no quietist and could never have meant that. Then, what does he mean by the phrase? And, of equal concern, how does one put trust in the strength of the Holy Spirit? Is this mere pious talk, or can the ways and means of trusting the Spirit's strength be set forth in practical terms?

- R.W. Dale: "The Christian who supposes that there are sins which the Holy Ghost cannot enable him to subdue, dishonors 'the exceeding greatness of his power' which worketh in all that believe. There is no sin for which Christ atoned from which He cannot deliver us. There is no sin that He can pardon which He cannot give us strength to overcome…I see His promises translated into facts." *Weekday Sermons*. London: Hodder & Stoughton (1834), pp. 108. 127.

    - o We all will admit that God can do such things; of that there is no doubt. But seeing these promises "translated into facts" Dale believes that what he says is not only theoretically possible, but also practically applicable to believers. We would like to know more about this "strength to overcome." What is it? Where may it be found? How can one obtain it? The statement about strength turned into facts in the lives of believers is tantalizing. Promises becoming facts? That's good! But how did they do it? And what, precisely, did they do?

- Bert Ghezzi: "If the Christian has been given a new nature as Scripture says, if he lives in the Spirit, if He has crucified the flesh, then he can live a new life. Many Christians think that they do not have the power or the resources to live a new life in Christ…The power is already in them and will make the change." *Pastoral Renewal*, September '79; Vol. 4, No 3, p. 22.
    - "If…if…if." Ah! More qualifications. But we ask, how…how…how? In what way is the "power" to lead a new life "within?" How does one "turn it on?" What are the "resources?" And, while we're at it, how does one "crucify the flesh?" Doesn't consideration of Galatians 2:20 make one wonder whether it is necessary to "crucify the flesh" since we have already been "crucified with Christ?"

- Andrew Murray: He urges the Christian to "say: 'Lord God, not a word upon my tongue but for thy glory, not a moment of my temper but for thy glory, not an affection of love or hate in my heart but for thy glory…'" Then he asks, "Do you think that is possible?" His answer: "What God has promised you, and what God can do to fill a vessel absolutely surrendered to Him…" is possible. *Absolute Surrender*. Chicago: Moody Press (nd), p. 14.
    - Whoa! If a person is already absolutely surrendered, then 1) would he need to seek the fulfillment of the promise? 2) God can do these things if He wills, granted. But how does one go about surrendering absolutely (i.e., flawlessly, completely non-sinfully)

unless he is already surrendered 100 percent? Is he saying that you must have it to get it?

- A.T. Robertson: "Preaching often is so given to denunciation of sin that it fails to exalt the possibilities of the right sort of manhood." *Studies in the Epistle of James.* NY: Doran (1915), p. 201.

    o That's true. But does "exalting" bring it about? And what does he mean by "the right sort of manhood?" Is he speaking of the same kind of thing as Illingworth, who promised true self-development?

- Manifesto: Coalition on Revival. 1986 (under "Essential Truths): Living Above Sin: "We affirm that it is possible and expected by God that Christians will and must live above conscious, deliberate choices to sin. We are capable of this because of our new nature [N.B.], the indwelling Holy Spirit and the ability of Christ's shed blood to break the power of cancelled sin."

    o How many Christians would sign a Manifesto like that? Is it true? Or, only potentially true? Has anyone ever lived a life like that? Does the Bible describe such people? What of Paul's known sin that he struggled with? He did, he says, the things that he didn't want to do. Is this pie in the sky? What do the words, "the ability of Christ's shed blood" mean? *How* does His blood's "ability" break the power of sin in a Christian's life?

- J.R.P. Salater: "When people left Christ's presence they did not shake their heads and say 'How high is the hill that we have to climb,' but 'We believe we shall really be able to climb this hill, steep as it is; and what's more, it will be worth it when we get to the top;" *The Public Worship of God.* NY: Doran (1927).

- o Define the hill, please! How do we get up it Have you known anyone who is king of the hill?

- Robert Murray M'Cheyne: "Paul was a new creature…we never hear of his slackening his pace.…He followed the Lord fully; he never looked back; he never halted; he never slumbered…" And then, of Caleb he wrote, "He had no inconsistencies – he followed the Lord in all he did. The most of Christians do not follow the Lord fully…" *Sermons.* London: The Banner of Truth Trust (1961), p. 128.

  - o What does he mean when he speaks of "following the Lord fully?" Without further explanation, this is confusing. Does he mean often, most of the time? It doesn't seem so. His words almost make Paul and Caleb out to be perfect persons, unlike the "most of Christians" who, according to M'Cheyne have "inconsistencies." Without taking anything away from the great man that God made him, is it helpful to set Paul up as virtually perfect? We all know that we are not, and it becomes discouraging to be told that we ought to be like him. Indeed, M'Cheyne goes on to say about us, "The most do not think it attainable." Well, if the standard is set so high why not give up in despair? But, wait! I thought Bible characters were men of "like passions" with ours. So, was Paul really so perfect? Remember his words in Romans 7. And Caleb – we read of one major event in his life, and have little else to evaluate him.

Is it right to say he "had no inconsistencies on the basis of so little evidence?" And wasn't he a partially sanctified person, who had difficulties with his life as we do? In other words, without many more qualifications, one wonders whether such claims help or hinder.

- James Reid: Speaking of one who supposedly had made it, Reid writes, "It is this complete commitment that makes it possible for God to shape and use us." *Living in Depth.* Edinburgh: The Saint Andrews Press (1959), p. 57.
  - Once again (though this time from a quite different source), we are told that God can't do anything for or with us until we totally surrender or – as Reid puts it – have made a "complete commitment." What does that mean? When one is completely committed is there no lurking doubt, sinful desire, failure to pray as we should, act of unfaithfulness *at all*? Knowing our own hearts, do we think that a "complete" commitment is possible? Or is he really describing something less than *true* completeness? If so, why doesn't he say so? Why doesn't he explain his terms? And, while we are asking questions, haven't we seen God "shape" our lives and even "use" us when we knew that we lacked total or complete commitment? Is this sort of talk misleading? Is it accurate? Is it helpful to realize that while we shall never attain to this completeness (in any reasonable sense of the word) a few ideal men did?

Now, all of these quotations were taken at random by pulling books off the shelves, thumbing through them, and typing them into the computer. Doubtless, "juicier" ones could have been found by searching, but I have long ago discarded most of the books that contain them. Yet even these, which are fairly innocuous, raise many questions, as I have endeavored to show. Consistently, the language used about the matter before us is loose, ill-defined, and often misleading. At best, writers ought to tighten up their concepts and the language that flows from them. Probably, few of the writers – Murray excepted – meant to speak in such absolute terms as they did. Pushed against the wall, most likely they'd begin qualifying. But, even so, why not qualify from the outset and avoid possible confusion?

Well, what next? Since so much that you read about SM is of this fuzzy or imprecise nature, it is my task to bring some sort of clarity to the matter. I recognize that I have set a difficult task before us. But it cannot be shirked if we wish to understand, plainly explain and apply the biblical teaching about SM.

7

But Wait a Moment!

There are other voices sounding from the church that want to put the brake on all such talk of SM. Indeed, some of them want to play down all exhortations to enter into life on a higher plane or anything remotely like it. They believe that there is no rainbow or – at least – no pot of gold. They interpret the Scriptures quite differently from the authors that we have just reviewed. They want to quash all hopes of great and dramatic change in a Christian's present life. Are these people Scrooges? In this chapter, we shall listen to what it is that they have to say.

According to Hamilton, the creedal statements of the Reformation got Protestants started on the dark side. He wrote:

> The Reformation went too far in pessimism. It concentrated on wickedness in human nature… we should follow the New Testament emphasis on the divine possibilities…rather than the negative Augustinian emphasis.

Sangster agrees:

> …the main stream of Protestant theology does not estimate highly man's ability to achieve (or receive) holiness in this life. Man is a sinner, a sinner dyed in the wool. He is always a sinner. There is sin not only in his vices but in his virtues. There is something to be forgiven in the best thing the best man did on the best day of his life.

These two Methodist writers have homed in on what they believe to be a serious fault of the Reformation creeds. Are they correct? In some ways yes; in others no. Certainly, they are correct in discerning a lack of enthusiasm for SM among the Reformers. R.W. Dale has this to add: "It is quite true that Christendom has encouraged a holy melancholy." But what does that mean? We will let the proponents of what we shall call the minimal view (over against the maximal view of persons like Andrew Murray) speak for themselves.

- Luther: "While we live in the flesh here on earth, we cannot attain such degree of perfection as to be free from weakness and imperfection." *Twentieth Century Preaching*. Fant and Pinson, Waco: Word (1974). p. 51.
    - But wait a moment, Martin. While we must agree that perfection is impossible here, what do you mean by the impossibility of "such a degree" of perfection? Isn't to speak of "perfection" like calling something unique, a term that, strictly speaking, allows for no degrees of comparison? It would seem that you are not speaking "strictly." Do you mean that the degree of advancement one can expect in his Christian experience is small? That seems to be the thrust of your remark. But to speak of weakness and imperfection in the same breath is really raising the bar, isn't it? Can't someone overcome weaknesses – at least to some extent? This needs clearing up!

- Calvin: "There will always be lurking within us some secret hypocrisy...we are yet far from perfection....Our works will always be tainted with some spot." *Sermons on Ephesians*. Edinburgh: The Banner of Truth Trust (1979), p. 433. Elsewhere, he declared, "For if we have a good aim an affection is upright in itself and approved by God, still we always raising something…For whatever virtues are in us God shows us vices in them in order that all pride may be abased…even the good is corrupted by the sin which dwells in us and of which we are filled to excess." *Sermons on the Saving Word of Christ*. Trans. –ed., Leroy Nixon. Grand Rapids: Baker (1980). pp. 58, 59.

- o "My, oh my, John," someone says. "Does that mean when we reach for something higher, what we get will always be messed up?" Well, yes. And it seems, therefore, anything "higher" cannot be that much higher after all. Pressing Calvin further, our inquirer says, "If all I can do is mess up, what sort of incentive does that give me for trying? It looks like no matter what I do I cannot please God." A serious objection to consider!

- Farmer: "We are never respectable in [God's] sight…the best righteousness of the best of us, in stark and literal fact … [is] filthy rags." *Things Not Seen*. Herbert Farmer, London: Nisbet (1929).
  - o Wow! If Farmer were speaking about the unsaved, of course, we'd readily agree. But saying that of the redeemed? Did regeneration count for nothing? Is it never possible to perform a single, untainted righteous act – even with the Spirit's help? Isn't that going pretty far? Why do we call them "righteous" if such acts are so unrighteous that they can be described as filthy rags? Well, then, is it possible that Andrew Murray could be right after all when he says "Don't let us think, because the blessed Reformation restored the great doctrine of justification by faith, that the power of the Holy Spirit was fully restored." He goes on to say that

there is "…a higher standard of spiritual life." Who is right – the maximalist or the minimalist?

- Jowett: Jowett approaches the matter from the standpoint of the church's classic hymnody: "Even many of the hymns which sing about the will of God are in a minor key, and they dwell upon the gloomier aspects of providence which calls for a state of resignation." *God our Contemporary*. NY: James Clarke (1922), p. 28.
    - Jowett not only suggests that there is a problem, but decries its dreaded effect – resignation. Is he correct? Aren't there many great hymns in the major key? Don't many of them rejoice over Christ's saving grace? Think of the Christmas carols, for instance. On the whole, they are joyful, aren't they?

- The Heidelberg Catechism (Answer to Q. 114): "…even the holiest of men, while in this life, have only small beginnings of this obedience, yet so, that with sincere resolution, they begin to live, not only according to some, but all the commands of God."
    - So, we have a not-so-great start at Christian living! And, that is supposed to be true of those who have abundant – eternal – life? Hmmm.

- The Apology for the Augsburg Confession: "…this fulfilling of the Law or obedience toward the Law, is indeed, righteousness when it is complete, but in us it is small and impure…these works are far distant from the perfection of the Law."
    - There it is again – "small." That seems to be a characteristic description of the minimalist view. All we are able to achieve, even with the Spirit working within, is but a small beginning. And even that is

"impure." Again, it looks like there is no way to please God since we always offer him an imperfect sacrifice! Are all Christians Cains rather than Abels?

- The Formula of Concord: This document insists that "regeneration and renewal are…in a constant struggle against he flesh, i.e., against the corrupt nature [M.B.] and disposition which cleaves unto us unto death."
    - Ah Ha! Sounds like Romans 7. But wait a moment! What is this corrupt nature? Are not believers regenerated? Are they not new creatures in Christ? How can these two concepts be squared?

- The Westminster Confession of Faith: After some positive remarks, the WCF asserts "…there abideth still some remnants of corruption in every part [of our good works]…so that the "best works are imperfect and defiled in the sight of God."
    - Then, why attempt the impossible? Why try to please God when we can't? But, hold on! Philippians 2:13 makes it clear that God Himself enables us to please Him. Can both statements somehow be true, or are they hopelessly contradictory?

Thus the Reformers, and their creedal documents are uniform, tilting heavily to the minimalist side; especially those by the Lutherans. Is it possible that this largely negative view of the regenerate, leading to an abandonment of SM, was the outgrowth of their emphasis on justification and not on sanctification, so that the latter was never explicated as it might have been? And did Luther begin a trend that, in time, permeated all Reformation thinking?

It will be interesting to attempt to reach an understanding, and perhaps even a synthesis, of the biblical elements in these diverse views. The maximal and minimal positions are distinct; there can be no doubt about that. But are they distinct at their cores? Is the seeming clash only a matter of semantics? We shall begin to investigate these subjects in the next chapter.

8

What Shall We Say?

What we have encountered shouts for clarification. Who is right/wrong? Should we side with the maximal or the minimal views? Or is there a third? In order to get our arms around the issue, let's begin by summing up what we've learned so far.

- Like others, Christians want SM.
- They recognize from experience, as well as from the Scriptures, that there must be more to the Christian life than the life many [most?] live.
- Christian authors and the Bible encourage such a yearning.
- Teachers of all sorts say, "You have a great God with unlimited resources that you haven't even begun to tap." But then some say, "There is a marvelous life of victory over sin just waiting for the taking. The Reformation emphasis about this matter is clearly wrong. You can have SM; you *can* live on a higher plane."
- Others, who also believe in God's "unlimited resources" and who think that Christians "haven't even begun to tap" them, nevertheless come to a very different conclusion. They say, "Yes, you can make some progress, but what you accomplish will be 'small' and 'impure.'"
- The maximalist, however, may adhere to an elitist view: that very few ever reach the coveted life of victory that they promise. They are always telling others about this

life, but they seem to think that there is a relatively small number of Christians who ever live it; perhaps, not even themselves.

- The minimalist, on the other hand, believes that all Christians advance – a bit – but come far short of what God requires. And, indeed, even the little that they do achieve is vitiated by sin.

- Is the maximalist an optimist and the minimalist a pessimist? No. Both believe that in the end all comes out right. Every true Christian will be perfected in eternity. This is true even for the maximalist's majority (who never seem to make it to the higher plane) and for all true Christians that the minimalist sees creeping along toward a goal way off in the distance.

- The maximalist teaches his disciple to look for change to take place instantaneously at some time subsequent to regeneration. This change may or may not be effected by a series of steps according to some formula. But, either way, it is an act; it is not a process. The act is given various names: absolute surrender, letting go and letting God, yielding, total commitment, the baptism of the Spirit, and a Second Blessing.

- Charles Solomon describes "Total Commitment" as "…an irrevocable decision in which we give God our permission to do anything He wishes in us, with us, to us or through us. We give up all our rights,"

- The minimalist looks for no instantaneous change following regeneration. The progress that is made toward victorious living is measured, slow, and never (even in one particular) complete. It is always marred and insufficient. This undue yearning for SM, therefore, must cease!

There can be no question about it: We are looking at two opposing views of the SM quest, and whether or not there should even be such a quest. We will begin to sort things out in the following chapter.

9

Basic Biblical Considerations

Before dealing with specifics, I want to consider some fundamental facts that have a bearing upon the two views that we are studying. Some may apply to both; others to but one.

First, in the entire corpus of epistles (including Jesus' epistles in Revelation 2 and 3), the writers deal with problems one-by-one. They do not handle them *en masse*. They don't call for one definitive, instantaneous action to do so. They expect *many* advances to take place over the period of one's lifetime. I Thessalonians 4:10 is a good example of this: "...indeed, you show love toward all the brothers....But we urge you, brothers, that you continue to do so more and more." On the contrary, instantaneous views tend to teach the opposite of Scriptural truth. For instance, a formula such as that taught by Keswick or by the Salvation Army, if followed to the hilt, we are told, in an instantaneous act will raise one to a higher level of living. Everyone is in the same boat prior to the event. And the "totally surrendered" are safely sequestered in their same boat afterwards. A person living on a level that is spiritually unproductive is virtually worthless to the work of God and miserable in himself. Take the step – yield – and all of this changes! It may happen at a meeting or in a bedroom, or anywhere he *yields*. That is the maximalist's solution.

In contrast, the minimalist sees no hope for a dramatic change in his lifestyle. Like all other Christians, he is slowly wending his way toward the goal of perfection which is so far off in the distance that it cannot easily be seen. Indeed, even the small advances that he makes are not really true advances since his deeds are so tainted by sin that he can do nothing well-enough to please God. Again, all are in the same boat; what is said of the one may be said of the other. It is a matter of living day by day in much the same way, making some sort of progress. That "progress" (with all of its impurities) may come in mini-surges or through gradual effort. But he himself must always be displeased with what he does or he may become proud. He cannot rejoice in large victories. Those minor victories that are forthcoming are merely a part of his ongoing way of life.

In contrast to a monolithic view of the Christian life, the Scriptures encourage work with specific problems such as lust, fear, jealousy, anger, envy, murder, hatred, gossip, and so forth. All persons are not treated as if they were on the same level. Biblical writers do not deal with *levels* of life – such as higher or lower planes. A person may grow more rapidly in one area than in another. Peter, for instance, says, "Make every effort to supplement your faith with virtue, and virtue with knowledge, and knowledge with self-control, and self-control with endurance, and endurance with godliness and godliness with brotherly kindness and brotherly kindness with love" (II Peter 1:5–7). Obviously, the idea of "supplementing" or "adding" communicates the idea of disparate progress in each of the areas listed.

It is also enlightening to note that, as naturally as one could expect, Peter goes on to say, "When these things are yours, and abound, they will keep you from becoming inactive or unfruitful with respect to the full knowledge of our Lord Jesus Christ" (v. 8). He doesn't say "let go and let God," and all of these things will be added to you. There is nothing of a one-time yielding that brings them about. And – don't miss this – one can have all of these things *and "abound in them."* That doesn't sound like slogging along, acquiring them little by little by means of miniscule, tainted successes.

It would seem, therefore, that both those who teach the one-time-act, and those who teach snail-like progress, have something to learn from the Bible. There is as much more variety and difference in the way that people change as there is in their dedication, their circumstances, and their personalities. People are not monolithic; the Scriptures don't treat them as if they were. Some sleep (Ephesians 5:14), many creep (Hebrews 12:12, 13), and others leap (I Thessalonians 1:5–10). If either of the one-solution-fits-all approaches were biblical, the Bible would be reduced to a few pages. There would be an explanation of the change dynamic postulated, a call to yield or to stop the vain pursuit for SM, and not much more. Keswick's five-day program could be taught on five pages of Scripture! Minimal, shoddy progress leaves little to learn. Since the Scriptures don't reduce all problems to one, they call for many different sorts of solutions. We have a Book, filled with problems of every sort, dealt with as such (consider I Corinthians). It is full of hope, rebuke, help, teaching, encouragement, guidance, commands, and the like. And the characters we meet in it are not Xeroxed copies of one another.

Second, Scripture indicates that believers will continue to sin. They are called to take up their crosses *daily*, put self to death, and follow Christ – as we have seen in an earlier chapter. Why is that a necessity if one is living on the higher plane of continual victory over sin? The Lord's prayer presupposes that brothers will have to ask and grant forgiveness of one another. Christians are encouraged to "pursue" righteousness. But why track it down as earnestly as a hunter (as the word "pursue" means)? Isn't it enough to yield? None of these facts seems to correspond to the "Get out of the way and let God do it for you instead of you" approach: of the maximalists. Charles Solomon's idea that "If He [God] is to take control, then we must lose control" sounds strangely suspicious when we find a Bible filled with exhortations to do this thing or that.

Third, consider this principle: the human and the Divine are said to work together in bringing about sanctification: "...that by the *Spirit's* sanctification *you* may obey" (I Peter 1:2). The Spirit works to set believers apart from sin to righteousness as they obey God's Word. Sanctification is a *joint venture* that requires action from both the divine and the human sides. Spirit-taught, Spirit-encouraged, and Spirit-enabled action pleasing to God is the picture presented in Philippians 2:13. If we are to "lose control," yield or "let God do it," then why is the Spirit needed to empower believers to obey? And, on the other side of the fence, if Christians are able to obey by the power of the Spirit, why are the results so minimal and tainted? The fact of the cooperative nature of sanctification seems to cut both ways, doesn't it?

Finally, one other basic principle: In Scripture, God never calls the Christian a "sinner." That doesn't mean he no longer sins, but it is interesting to note that there is a significant difference in the way that God views believers and unbelievers. Christians are called "saints' (set-apart ones), "new creatures," "the children of God," "believers," and the like. The positive change that occurred when they were regenerated is what is emphasized. To apply passages like Jeremiah 17:9 ("the heart is deceitful and desperately wicked") to a believer, as some do to buttress the idea that all efforts of believers are impure, is an error. This is true especially when God plainly says that the Christian has a new heart (Jeremiah 31:33; Ezekiel 36:25–27). Confusing passages concerning believers, with those dealing with unregenerate persons, is a serious exegetical mistake which largely accounts for the notion that man can do little, and less that is good.

Take to heart these preliminary thoughts that seem to cut both ways. Ponder them because in the next two chapters I shall enlarge upon them with specific reference first, to the maximal view and then to the minimal approaches.

10

Dimming the Glare

The bright view takes several forms, which are not altogether the same and do not promise exactly the same things; it is true. Nevertheless, they are similar enough to consider in their broad aspects, and in contrast to Reformation teaching, they *all* hold out the promise of maximal change in the present life.

As a reminder of what we have already considered, let me distinguish the four principal forms of the maximal view:

1. Sinless Perfectionism in which sanctification, like regeneration, is instantaneous. "You can have it now, if you only will." These maximalists believe that one can attain to sinless perfection in this life.

2. Higher Life (or Victorious living). The idea is to yield as you consecrate yourself to God. He will take over and live His life through you.

3. GFI – a ministry of Charles Solomon. In an irrevocable act of total commitment, one "lets loose" of the control of his life and asks God to take over instead. Self is thus hindered from its place in the heart.

4. Charismatic, Pentecostal, and Salvationist views. These views come in many shapes and flavors, but all of them believe in some sort of "Second Work of Grace." This second blessing, following regeneration, is the common thread that groups them together.

Bright (or maximal) views are reductionistic. That means in their eyes, all problems seem to meld into one (usually self, pride, or something akin to them). Once the believer gets out of the way and let's God take over, or receives a second blessing, he is lifted to a realm of existence in which, at last, he is able to victoriously suppress sin.

In addition, bright views are ordinarily quietistic; i.e., passive. Once yielded, God alone is responsible for one's actions. This removal of the individual Christian's responsibility, however, is extremely dangerous. It tends to "put him to sleep" spiritually. In his spiritual stupor, in one way or another, he is able to dismiss responsibility for sin. Like perfectionists, he may tend to rename sins as "mistakes," acts of "immaturity," and so on. And his standard for what is sin may be lowered.

Quietism is opposed to 'self help" views in which one must pull himself up by his own bootstraps. No major Christian theology holds to that view, however. But the maximalist sets it up as the belief of those he opposes and sounds quite pious in his denunciation of "self-helpism." Over against this straw man, he waxes eloquent about how, in contrast to those who rely on self rather than on God, he has totally surrendered his all to Him. But the problem here is that, as I said, those who differ with bright side doctrines don't ignore God in the process of sanctification. Indeed, they call on Him to enable them to do those things that please Him (Philippians 2:13). They just heartily disagree with the all-too-sunny approach of maximalists to the doctrine of sanctification. In their eyes, it is so glaring a mistake that they think all should be able to see through it.

Consider a problem: In Hebrews 5:11–6:1, the writer chides lethargic Hebrew Christians who had stopped *maturing* in their faith (6:1). Worse still, they had retrogressed. What was the problem with these backsliding Christians? They had ceased progressing in their understanding and appropriating of biblical teaching. Like a baby, content to hang on to his bottle when it's time to lay it aside for food, these Christians were contented to suck on the elementary truths of Christianity. As a result, they not only failed to grow; they became "dull" of hearing. What was the solution?

Obviously, the writer of Hebrews, being a maximalist, recommended the simple bright side solution to their problem: Stop trusting in yourself and yield your life entirely to God. Right? Wrong! He did no such thing. Instead of pointing them to some instantaneous "experience" that would lift them out of their sin to joyous Christian living, he urged repentance, followed by "training" (5:14), growth through feeding on "solid food" (5:13) and "maturation" in order to go on from the first principles to others as well (6:1). There isn't a word about finding the solution to the lethargy of these Christians through some crisis experience! As elsewhere in the Bible, both quietistic and second-work-of-grace maximalism is foreign to the passage.

Again, in the case referred in Hebrews, no single act is recommended. Training in Scripture, leading to the experienced application of it to life, is the answer. But that is a time-consuming thing. Even the brightsiders don't believe that this can be acquired instantly. It requires constant study and application of truth.

And, it is apparent that what led them to retrogress was not a failure of the consecration of the self. To the contrary, what occasioned the "dullness" to which they had become accustomed was the failure to grow through greater knowledge and application of God's Word to their daily lives. They no longer "heard" the truth of God because they had ceased living according to it. "Learn more of Scripture" hardly sounds like the advice the Salvationist or Andrew Murray would give these sinning believers.

As we have seen in our earlier discussion of life that is abundant (John 10:10), there is no *call* to abundant living. Rather, there is but a factual statement that the abundant life Jesus came to bring is here. He does not urge them to enter into it. Certainly, then, there is no thought in the passage of classes of sheep that lead two very different sorts of lives – one life that is abundant and one that is mundane. The fact of the matter is that the life that Jesus brought to His people is eternal life – life that is more joyous, productive, God-honoring – life that is *always* like that. It doesn't change. The change must take place in the saint who avails himself of it more and more.

It is sad to see people duped into thinking that by some instantaneous act they can soar to spiritual heights above others. They may soar in their minds for a time, but even there, it is not very long before they come plummeting down to earth! Many who have accepted this view have learned the sad consequences the hard way. They had their hopes flying high only to come crashing down around their feet. We meet people like this in our counseling rooms. They are defeated, dispirited, who after yielding time and again, find that no victorious life experience was forthcoming. Like Packer, they found that it just didn't happen.

When persons who have failed to experience the contentment and satisfaction promised by GFI come for help, we often find it necessary to deal with them in a particular way. Since many are still filled with the notion that God must take over and completely control their lives, and that any effort they make to bring about change is purely fleshly and not God-honoring. We must disabuse them of the idea. We uphold their concern to honor God, but the idea of shirking their responsibility must be discouraged.

So, how do we counter that view? We say, "Go home this week and study the Book of I Corinthians. As you do so, on a paper with three columns, head each with a separate title. Column one: Command; column two: the Holy Spirit (or God in you); column three, the Corinthians (or, yourself). Now as you come across a command, write it out in the first column. Then, in the second or third column check off who is commanded to obey it. If they don't get the point as the assignment is given, and actually go home and do it, they will return with their pages filled with check marks in the third column with none in the second. Obviously, the thrust of the homework is to get them to see that they are not to passively sit back, expecting God to do for them what He has commanded them to do.

Failure to come to grips with the truth of the Bible in regard to a Christian's responsibility to obey God will lead to failure in learning to appropriate more of the abundant life that Christ brought. It is always available; but they must make every effort to avail themselves of it!

11

Solar Eclipse?

At the outset of the last chapter, I listed four prominent bright side views together because of the slight differences between them. Here, there is no need for a similar list. As you have doubtless noted from the selections quoted, the Reformation creedal statements are virtually identical. What do they teach?

Four Facts About Minimalism

First, minimalists hold that there is no such thing as an instantaneous event that explodes into abundant or victorious living. They are absolutely correct in debunking this non-biblical teaching.

Second, every work that promotes the kingdom of God and is formally righteous by biblical standards is seriously marred by the fact that it is tainted by sin. *Nothing* a believer does can completely satisfy God, and the minimalist must recognize that fact if he would be free from pride. This view gives rise to some difficulties.

Third, minimalists concede the fact that there *is* growth in Christian living that does tap into the abundance that Jesus brought. But what a believer receives is not all that much, no matter who the Christian may be. He will not make significant progress in his present life.

Fourth, the minimalists correctly teach that there are not two classes of Christians, one that lives on a higher plane than the other. All are at some point on the same continuum, or plane, of existence.

More facts might be mentioned, but I shall go with these four items since they are of the greatest significance in understanding the minimalist viewpoint.

I quickly want to dispose of the two-class doctrine that places Christians on distinct levels of existence. The Scriptures know nothing of any such thing. It is pure invention. In rejecting this teaching the minimalists could not be closer to the truth. Later, in Chapter 16, I shall fully consider this matter.

Saints or Sinners?

Earlier, I mentioned the fact that more than sixty times God calls the Christian a "saint" in the Scriptures. That doesn't mean that he is "saintly" (in the popular sense of the word), but that God has set him apart from unbelievers to become a part of His own people. Scripture doesn't call or characterize him as a sinner; in the Bible, he is never named such. Rather, he is called a child of God, making it clear that he belongs to the family of which Jesus Christ is the elder brother. He is said to be a part of the body of Christ, the church. And the Bible affirms the fact that he has become a new creation. That is to say, God has regenerated him so that he has a new life now oriented toward God and righteousness, even though he does not always do those things that he now desires to accomplish for God's glory. Those are givens in the Scriptures. Minimalists downplay these facts when discussing the issue before us.

Imperfect Works?

There is some confusion that results from the minimalist position on the inability of the believer to perform even one act that is entirely pleasing to God. One cannot help wondering about such passages as Ephesians 2:10. There, the Christian is said to be God's "handiwork, created in Christ Jesus for good works, that God prepared beforehand so that we might walk in them." Questions arise.

How can it be that works prepared by God are so tarnished as to shame us enough to reduce any vestiges of pride in them? Did God actually "prepare" tainted and impure works for the believer? If, so, then when Paul calls them "good works" is he fudging? Are they really "good" if they are so greatly marred? How could they be said to be so? Indeed, Heppe goes so far as to say that good works are sins." Or, is it possible that Paul was speaking only of the formal aspect of these works–that is, that outwardly they conform to God's standards, but inwardly they do not? But, then, could it not be said that some of the works of unregenerate persons also outwardly conform? Paul's description of his pre-conversion lifestyle seems to prove that possible (Philippians 3:6). Is the difference that their works are displeasing to God because they have but the "form of godliness, but deny the power thereof?" Now, wait a minute! Something is wrong here – good works are "sins?"

"Fine Deeds" or Not?

Now, consider this: when the Christian is said to be "created in [or by] Christ Jesus for good works," does that mean that he was created to perform works that are not really good in the full sense of that term, but only *sort of* good? Can we really believe that God recreated His own to perform works that He only partially approves of? There seem to be quite serious difficulties here that have not been addressed adequately by the minimalists. While the minimalists may call themselves realists, who take into account the devastating effects of sin upon man, can they escape the many texts that call redeemed man to various good works that are never called "tainted" by the New Testament writers? Take for instance Titus 2:14: where God says that He wants His children to be "a people zealous for fine deeds." If so marred by sin, why call them "fine?"

And, in this regard, don't miss Titus 3:8 in which Paul says, "so that those who have believed in God may make it their business to engage in fine deeds." Notice, again, the translation "fine deeds." The word in the original is *kalos* not *agathos*. The latter means good, as over against bad; the former is "fine" as over against that which is poor, shoddy. How can "fine deeds" be said to be "defiled and mixed with so much weakness and imperfection that they cannot endure the severity of God's judgment?" And, as a final comment, what about Enoch who was removed so as not to see death? The book of Hebrews says, "Before the removal he had received the testimony that he was well-pleasing to God" (Hebrews 11:6). Are well-pleasing works so miserable that from *any* perspective they may be viewed as "sins?"

No Artificial Division

It does not help matters to say that what the Spirit contributes to a deed is perfect but what a Christian contributes is defiled. Scripture doesn't separate the two. To try to do so is academic and unwarranted. There is only one "deed" in the picture in Titus and elsewhere – the deed that the Christian did aided by the Spirit. And it, in its combined aspects – its unity – is said to be "fine." Paul did not say that the element contributed by the Spirit would be fine and that contributed by the saint would be defiled. This analysis is entirely artificial. And what he says of "fine deeds" in Titus holds true of what he calls "good works" in Ephesians! While the biblical picture is not so glaringly bright as the other's is, it isn't a solar eclipse either! It seems that it is a good bit brighter than that presented by the minimalist, don't you think?

J. I. Packer recognizes the minimalist's problem, agrees with his viewpoint, but offers no solution other than to tone down his emphasis on sin in the believer:

"Scripture supports Augustinianism [the Reformation view]...but censures many Augustinians for making too much of our continuing sinfulness and too little by comparison of the scriptural expectations of ongoing moral change into Christ's image through the Holy Spirit."

How Far?

Now, for the matter of how far one can progress in his Christian life – must he never even get near the godly destination that he has in mind? Is it really out of sight? Can he not see it from afar? The minimalist boards the plane. It is filled with fuel, the motors are running, the pilot revs them up, and everyone tightens his seat belt. But nothing happens. There he sits on the tarmac. Eventually, the plane may taxi out onto the runway, but it never takes off. That seems to be the picture the minimalists present. Isn't it closer to the biblical presentation to say that the plane is airborne, travels toward its destination, and in some cases at least, finally comes into sight of the landing field? It is true that he never reaches his destination in this life, but he can look down at the countryside passing beneath him and see that he is en route. He sees definite progress. In this regard, see Philippians 3:12–15!

Acts of Faith

Not only do the expectations of the Bible seem to be more than minimal, but its declarations about those who have lived a life of faith before God do so as well. Can we rightly characterize the acts of the saints in Hebrews 11 as minimal? Were their actions so far from the goal that they could not "endure the severity of God's judgment?" I am not talking about any individual's life as a whole. Sure, there is still plenty of sin in all of us this side of heaven. But, I ask, "What of particular acts of faith here or there? Was every one of these so tainted that it could not pass judgment? Has no one in all of the world's history (Jesus excepted) ever done an entirely righteous act?" Even one? If not, then why speak of "the righteous" as the Bible does – when there is no such person? Does every verse in which that word occurs refer to imputed righteousness? All those in Proverbs? Hardly. There is something wrong here that needs serious rethinking.

Where did this thinking come from? It is difficult to know, but one possibility is that the negative perspective grows out of the application of biblical descriptions of the unregenerate to the regenerate. Some of the Puritans did this in their sermons and expositions. Packer thinks that "The basic problem is that right from the start Augustinians, being confronted with ideas of self-generated merit…have couched their belief that no human action in this world is quite perfect in terms that sound ethically negative and pessimistic to the last degree." Certainly this description of these minimalist "terms" seems accurate. But whatever the origin of this very pessimistic view of the regenerate, it must be reconsidered.

In reconsidering the "Augustinian" view, as Packer calls it, two things must be paramount. First, in no way may sinless perfectionism or victorious life dogmas be accepted in its place. The idea that even the regenerate can live above sin belies all that Paul writes in Romans 6 and 7. There, he exhorts the believer to fight against the sinful patterns that he adopted in his pre-conversion life and brought over into the new life in Christ. His message? This inconsistency must end (cf. Romans 6:1ff.)! The fact that the believer has a body habituated to sin must be fully acknowledged and dealt with. Stephen Neill writes, "There is a tendency among Christians not to take seriously enough the power of habit…the Christian enters on his Christian experience with innumerable habits already formed." For details about this, see my *Winning the War Within*.

Pleasing God

Now, an important fact that must be maintained at all costs is that it is possible for the believer to do things that please God.

That God is pleased with acts that are so tainted they would not pass His scrutiny seems strange in light of the many passages in which believers are called upon to do things that please Him. Note, especially, Hebrews 13:21 where in his benediction, the writer expressly says that God will "equip [us] with every good thing for doing His will, *producing in us what pleases Him* through Jesus Christ." Does He do so or not? Are tainted works "pleasing" to God? I don't think so. Whatever other ideas one has, it seems clear that he must believe that it is possible for the believer to please God.

12

Who's Right?

Is it the maximalists who see the sun shining brilliantly in a blue sky where there isn't a single cloud? Or is the minimalists who have difficulty making out the stars at night time because of the haze? The answer is, neither. The plane must take off and it does make progress (how much, depends on the flight you take and the airline you fly); but it never lands. Given the condition of the equipment available, that is remarkable. You've boarded a beat up old aircraft that has flown the hump! Only recently has it been refitted and refurbished for flight. But there is yet much work to do to make it the plane it was designed to be. Nevertheless, enough repairs have been made to enable it to fly slowly and safely.

What am I trying to say? In plain English just this: Both viewpoints contain elements of truth. The minimalist says that none will reach perfection here. He's right. The maximalist says, "Ah, but he will make significant progress." He's right (depending on what you mean by "significant").

Well, what then shall we say about the quest for SM? Is it valid? Is it worthwhile? Will it be productive? Is there a rainbow to chase, and (if so) is there a pot of gold at its end? The answer is "no" to all of those questions. The supposed rainbow was a mirage. The chase will end in frustration – or worse! There is no validity to the idea that there is SM for the Christian to obtain. His efforts to discover it will be wasted.

Well, then, if that is true, why is it that so many Christians have a yearning for SM? Have they been deceived? Are they like the world, just plain dissatisfied with life? Why the desire for SM? The simple response, that I shall try to work out in the rest of this book, is that Christians don't need SM. The yearning is real. There is genuine need. What they need is not *Something More*, but

more of the something they already have!

13

The Path of the Righteous

OK, so you didn't like my airplane analogy – it was too much like an allegory in which you had to make all sorts of uncertain applications. If so, then I have another for you. But this is one I know you will like, because it is God's! Think about these words from Proverbs 4:18:

> But the path of the righteous is like the morning light
> That gets brighter and brighter until it is noonday.

In contrast, the writer tells us: "The way of the wicked is like thick darkness; they don't know what they stumble over" (Proverbs 4:19). Now, at the heart of verse 18 is the idea of progress. Even John Calvin, who said, "…we are so corrupted that we cannot use our senses in any manner whatever, nor apply them to anything except there would be some relic of our evil corruption displeasing to God," commenting on John 10:10 is forced to say, "…the greater progress that any man makes in faith, the more nearly does he approach to the fullness of life, because the Spirit, who is *life*, grows in him."

So, while holding to the view that there is no instantaneous, glorious change, not all minimalists think that significant change is impossible. Calvin, who understood "fullness of life" to mean precisely what I have been saying about "abundant [eternal] life," when commenting on John 10:10 mentions both progress and growth. It is those two aspects of the one truth taught also in Proverbs 4:18 that must be emphasized. There should be no ambivalence about both the possibility and the actuality of progress and growth in believers.

Light on the Pathway

In the proverb quoted above, progress is the dominant thought. When the newly born saint starts on his journey in Christ it is early morning. He has set out at the crack of dawn. The light is dim, he can see his way, but not clearly. He is yet unable to sharply delineate many of the objects that lie before him. So, if he is wise, he will move cautiously and slowly. However, as light increases in strength, he is able to make greater progress since he now is able to more clearly identify things about him. As he travels, the day grows brighter and brighter. At last, it is high noon and he walks more rapidly and more surely toward the ultimate goal of heavenly perfection! That is the ideal of the Christian life.

Now, of course, there are mistaken turns, times when he wanders off the path and gets into trouble, and so on. Sadly, the Christian may find himself in the shadows as well as in the light. That is why John has to urge us to "walk in the light" (I John 1:17). The Old and New Testaments are replete with warnings and calls to repentance for us all. But despite the inevitable ups and downs, the overall course of a true believer's life could be charted as an inclined plane. There is always progress in the life of a *true* Christian. There is, however, one significant word that Calvin used that we must not miss: it is "relic." We must explore it.

The Relic

When he speaks about the relic, Calvin identifies this "left over" as the remains of 'our evil corruption." He also defines it as "some relic of the infection which is from the womb of the mother." It seems certain, therefore, that he thinks the "corruption" remaining in the believer is a remnant of original sin. That would mean that the "new creation," unlike the first creation, is far from perfect. Does God create imperfect things?

How, then, does it differ from what it was before regeneration? Indeed, he leaves the nature of the change indefinite. What Scripture teaches is that what has changed is the inability of the unregenerate to please God (Romans 8: 8), as regenerate persons, they now can.

Everyone in the minimalist camp believes that something remains and is carried over into the new life in Christ. The idea of the relic is universal. With that fundamental assumption, I heartily agree. But not all believe that what remains is relics of original sin. Just what this "relic" of the past may be is a point of concern because it has much to do with how one progresses and how fully he may grow. It is *the* issue in sanctification.

There seems to be a strange sort of inconsistency (or tension) in Calvin. This tension comes to the surface as he writes, "…there is an amazing corruption in our natures; yet we must not lose courage, but let us always walk further…let us always have our senses focused higher…though there may be wicked affections, they may be held as it were in check, indeed enchained…that we may always remain firm." Thus, the nature seems unchanged except for a new ability to hold sinful propensities in check. That concept is quite different from the biblical idea of replacing (putting off and putting on) the old with the new. It is plainly about *replacing* that Ephesians and Colossians speak, not holding the old in check. So, his solution to the problem of SM is to recognize that our natures are yet full of sinful remains that we must reign in as much as possible. No wonder he cautions the reader not "to lose courage!" That is hardly an encouraging message!

Those who disagree that bits and pieces (or large chunks) of original sin remain in the believer's regenerate nature do so because they see in the saint the ability to "walk in newness of life" (Romans 6:4). To walk in newness of life is to walk in and by that abundance of life that Jesus Christ brought at His coming. That is to say, it is to avail one's self of all that Jesus provided for us by grace. And, we must not forget, "Where sin abounded, grace far more abounded" (Romans 5:20). It is possible to access things that pertain to the abundant life because the reign of sin over us has been broken. Where "sin reigned," through [spiritual] death, now grace reigns through righteousness, "resulting in eternal life" (Romans 5:21). In other words, sin no longer has authority over the believer; he has been set free from his cruel taskmaster (Romans 6:1). Regeneration has removed the believer from his former slavery to original sin. Now he has a new master; he is capable of righteousness (Romans 6:20, 21). The strange contention of Calvin is that regeneration is but partial: "Let us learn that though by nature we are entirely given to evil, and although God may have regenerated us in part, still our flesh does not cease to chafe against God," Why, then, do Christians still sin?

Why Christians Sin

The answer to that question is given in Romans 6: believers sin because they go on living as though they were still under the authority of sin. The story is told – I forget by whom and concerning whom – about a man recently discharged from the military. Upon leaving the base in his civilian clothes, he happened to pass his former commanding officer. Before he could think, he raised his hand to his forehead in a snappy salute. As he went a few more paces, it suddenly dawned on him, "I don't have to salute him any longer – I'm no longer under his authority!"

Christians are like that. Having been freed from the authority of sin, they go on living as if it had not happened. They go on practicing the habits that they learned while under sin's reign, often without giving conscious thought to what they are doing. That is why Paul wrote, "Don't let sin reign in your mortal body, with the result that you obey its desires" (Romans 6:12). These bodily desires have been deeply etched into us by years of service to sin. We want to do what we are used to doing. Christians are like the civilian, who was no longer under military authority and had to learn new ways appropriate to his new position. Throughout Romans 6, Paul is urging precisely that. He calls the Christian to live a life that is in accord with his new status and his new state. He is no longer reckoned a sinner: he is counted "dead to sin." Rather than thinking or living like the sinner that he once was, he should now be "living for God in Christ Jesus" (Romans 6:11). Let him do so is Paul's message. It is a freeing one. We are no longer forced to sin; we can advance in righteousness as we replace sinful life patterns with their righteous alternatives. What a joy to know this!

As you can see, there is a great difference between "reigning in" sinful propensities and "replacing" sinful habits with new holy ones! It is the difference between repressing sinful habits or replacing them. Think about it for a moment; the difference is truly significant. Would you rather make progress by presenting your body to God for His righteous service or continually strain to advance by holding down relics of original sin for the rest of your life? The first is positive, the second negative. While we must daily put our desires to death, we must also learn to follow Christ.

It is true that these bodily members have been serving sin for so long, that they want ["desire" to] go on doing it. Habits soon become "second nature." Believers sin because they continue to present the member of their bodies for sin's service. However, Paul says it's time for all of that to change, since one's status and capability have changed. Now, it is time to present the members of the body to righteousness for its service (Romans 6:13, 19). But, although this is a struggle, as Paul indicates in Romans 7:15ff., the hope of lasting change comes from the fact that the Holy Spirit dwells within, empowering the Christian to make the transition (Romans 8). Paul wrote: "Moreover, if the Spirit of the One Who raised Jesus from the dead dwells in you, this One Who raised Christ Jesus from the dead will give life to your mortal bodies through His Spirit Who dwells within you" (Romans 8:11). Throughout Romans chapters 6 through 8, Paul has been speaking about how, through habituation to sinful ways, the body has become a difficult problem for the believer. But in Romans 8:11, he says that God gives "life to your mortal bodies through His Spirit Who dwells within you" (Romans 8:11). He means the Christian's "body of death" (Romans 7:24) has been given spiritual "life" to be able to serve God *now*. The converse is also true: "by the Spirit" we may also "put to death [our] bodily practices" (Romans 8:13). So, the key here is this: because of regeneration (God's grant of "newness of life"), we have been freed from sin's rule and power and may exchange the slavery of the bodily practices to sin for the freedom of a glorious slavery to righteous ones (Romans 6:19–23).

So, what is the relic that troubles believers? Is it remnants of original sin? That is nowhere taught in the Scriptures. Rather, we are assured that we have been freed from the dominion of original sin. Then, how does sin affect us? That it does, we all know. We certainly don't have to be reminded of the fact!

The relics that are our problem are the habituated ways of thinking and doing that were ingrained in us while serving sin. These may be replaced by presenting our bodily members to God (Romans 6:13). Thus, instead of understanding Romans 12:1 as some sort of special, isolated (nearly magical) act in which one "yields" and rises to new heights, Paul's words in this chapter should be considered further elaboration of his words in chapters 6 through 8 about presenting (yielding) one's bodily members to righteousness. In the light of the argument in those three chapters, the verb here must be understood as an inceptive aorist, meaning "to begin presenting." It is not a once-for-all action. There is to be growth over time to come. But growth is a subject of its own that we will take a look at in the next chapter.

14

Growth Is the Right Metaphor

As he closed his second letter, Peter put it this way: "But grow by the help [grace] and the knowledge of our Lord Jesus Christ" (II Peter 3:18). In a letter in which Peter is thinking of his death and of leaving a heritage of truth behind for his readers, this commandment can be construed no other way than to say that it is highly significant. It was his last will and testament.

In Romans 8 and Galatians 5, as we have seen, Paul uses the metaphors of walking and leading. These correspond to the Proverbs passage that speaks about God's light shining more and more upon the path of the righteous. But growth is another, even more powerful analogy used to depict what spiritual progress is all about. All of these metaphors, you will notice, speak of an on-going process rather than an act. Perhaps the metaphor that portrays this progress most clearly is growth.

The Ideal: Spiritual Maturity

When James sets forth the proper goal of the Christian, he says that it is to become an *aner teleion* ("complete man"). By this he means a person who is "complete and entire, lacking in nothing" (James 1:4). The word "perfect," found in the KJV is misleading. The idea behind *telios* is a person who is mature in every area of his life. In Job 1:1, the parallel Hebrew word, *tam* has exactly the same meaning. Such a person, as we say today," has it all together." In other words, biblical growth is progress toward spiritual completion – or maturity – in every aspect of life. James says there is no area that should be deficient. Now, of course, no Christian ever reaches full maturity in all areas of his life, but if there is movement toward it in each – social, physical, commercial, educational, financial, ecclesiastical, marital, that is what James is hoping to see in his readers. In Ephesians 4:15, Paul (echoing the same sentiment) said he wanted his readers to "grow up in all respects." He was concerned that, instead, they might remain "infants" (v. 14); or grow in some, but not all, aspects of life. His concern for the members of the church was for them to arrive at "the unity of the faith and the full knowledge of God's Son, to mature manhood, to the point where [they would] become as fully adult as Christ." So, the idea for the Christian life is not something abstract; it is to become like Christ. He is the truly mature One. And, as a sidebar, it is important to note that as one member grows, so too does the entire body (v. 16).

Dull Christians

Now, the writer of Hebrews was concerned about the lack of growth in his readers (Hebrews 5:11–14; 6:1). Because they had not grown as they should have by that time, he observes that they had become "dull" of hearing (the word dull is a strong term that can be used to describe one in a coma). They lacked the sensitivity to truth that comes only from experienced users of the Word of truth. In other words, the only way to grow strong in Christ is through learning and practicing the teachings of God's Word. Because they lacked this stability, they were doubting their faith and wondering whether it might not be better to return to Judaism! From this informative passage, we can see how vital growth is to one's faith!

Fruit-Bearing

Growth is gradual; if anything refutes the view that mature spirituality is an instantaneous, crisis event, it is the idea of growth. Growth is progressive. It takes time and cultivation. No one ever put together a watermelon in a day – not even a grape! Fruit (the purpose of growth so prominent in Galatians 5) takes time to grow. And, to reap large, luscious fruit, there is the need for cultivation. That is why the Lord, Who desires "much fruit" (John 15:5), "prunes" His followers (v. 2) and urges them to "remain" (or "stay") in Him. He is the vine, they the branches. The branches draw their life from the vine.

Again, notice the progressive nature of fruit-bearing: "He prunes every branch that does bear fruit so that it may bear more fruit" (v. 2). God is not satisfied with fruit; He wants more – and more. That concept, as does the whole concept of growth and fruit-bearing, scuttles the notion that what pleases God is a one time experience. As in Hebrews 5, we see that it is the "Word" of Christ (now found in the Scriptures) that prunes out of the life of the believer those things that would hinder the production of large quantities of fruit. How important, then, is the study and the application of biblical truth to maturity in the faith.

The Word's Place in Growth

This maturity of growth that comes from the Word is mentioned in II Peter 3:18, quoted at the beginning of this chapter. Peter's parting words not only urge us to grow by God's grace (help), but also through "the knowledge of our Lord Jesus Christ." Knowledge of God's truth is essential to growth. The believer who is "untaught" in the things of God, Peter says, is "unstable" and is liable to "twist" the Scriptures. Tragically, Scripture-twisting is apparent in many of the writings that pour forth from Christian publishers today. The sermons that you hear on TV or radio often reflect much of the same immature thought and error. How sad, then, that some believe maturity can come about apart from the cultivation of fruit by hard labor and pruning through the Word. Today, the church of Christ suffers as much as anything from a lack of the knowledge of Christ. That is to say, of the truth about Him and His ways.

The idea of *advancing* inheres in the concept of growth: One must "leave behind" the elementary truths of the faith (not in order to abandon them, but to go beyond them) and "advance toward maturity" (Hebrews 6:1). Again, maturity is set forth in terms of knowledge (kneaded into the dough of life). It is the "elementary teachings" that one must "leave" (in the sense of focusing on them to the neglect of others) in order to learn those teachings that are more advanced. The writer would like to have discussed many of these with his readers but found that he couldn't at this point because of their dullness (Hebrews 5:11).

A Reason for Dullness

There are those today who are content to know as little as possible; for them it takes too much effort to grow in the knowledge of Jesus Christ. They will not expend the time or effort required. That is why they have become, like the Hebrews, "dull of hearing." Try to converse with them about important biblical matters and they are not interested. They pass off vital truth as if it were of little consequence. No wonder they don't grow! No wonder they are "unstable!" Their spirituality suffers because they fail to experience the pruning of the Word that they so desperately need!

A Christian without a library containing basic Christian books is probably a weak Christian. One who never touches a concordance or Bible dictionary probably understands very few truths. It is not Scriptural to talk about "more kneeology and less theology" as some of these negligent believers do. That phrase sounds pious, but it is close to heresy! How can one possibly commend "less theology" (knowledge about God and His ways) without bordering on heresy? While prayer is important, it is but a one-way street: talking to God. The believer must also *listen* to Him. And there is only one way to do so – through hearing Him speak by His written Word. The Scriptures *are* God's Word. And, when you think of it, which is more important – what you say to God or what He has to say to you?

More about Fruit

Fruit is an important biblical concept. Not only is it mentioned in Galatians 5 and John 15, but also in Luke 3:8, 9 and elsewhere, in which passages we see how important it is in the lives of new converts. After repenting, believing in the coming Messiah, and affirming their faith through baptism, John's new disciples rightly wanted to know what was next. "What shall we do?" was their question. John did not say, "Pray for a Second Blessing." He didn't hold a five-day Keswick conference. Nor did he talk about reigning in the relics of original sin. Instead, he spoke about their lives in terms of the daily changes that can actually take place: give clothes to the needy, live honestly in the future, don't take advantage of your authority and power, and stop griping about your wages. These are lifestyles that needed changing by replacing them with new ones – as John said! His concern was for "fruit" that is "fit for repentance."

What Causes Growth

We have seen from Peter, Paul, and the writer of Hebrews that knowing and appropriating God's truth for daily living causes men to grow spiritually. It is through His Word that God maintains a connection between the believer and Himself. Because of this, in the Garden of Eden, Satan aimed his attack at God's Word. His goal was to cut the connection and thus alienate man from God. The vital relationship of the Word to growth is seen in the image we have been considering – the vine and the branches. The healthy growth of the branch and a steady production of fruit is the result of that connection. In a slightly different, but closely related figure, the psalmist noted that the man whose "delight is in the law of the Lord" in which "he meditates day and night" is like "a tree planted by streams of water, that yields its fruit in its season, and its leaf does not wither" (Psalm 1:2, 3). Again, growth is inseparably united to the Bible.

Meditation, in the Scriptures, is not like Eastern meditation. God wants His people to mediate not upon themselves, the universe, or some nameless void, but upon His Word. Nor is it merely some sort of inner turning over of truth so as to digest it more thoroughly. No. Meditation goes beyond rumination. One who meditates well begins with a clear understanding of biblical truth. He then considers some aspect of his life in the light of that truth, making every effort to discover how the two relate to one another. He goes on to determine how that truth should change his living and ends with a plan to put it into effect. Edmund Smith says, "meditation is thinking ahead. It is making plans and taking definite action." Meditation, when properly carried out, is productive of fruit – "in its season!" The picture in Psalm 1 is of a well-supplied tree. The tree is healthy (its leaf doesn't wither) and it is productive because it is planted by the river (streams) of water. Let the dry seasons come, let the sun parch the earth; no matter! This tree has an unending supply of water. So, too, is the one whose life is firmly rooted in the Word of God. He has all he needs to remain strong and healthy in difficult times and to produce fruit regularly (in his season). He produces in no sporadic fashion, but when expected! That sort of disciplined and steady lifestyle is the result of daily ("day and night") mediation upon the Scriptures. Erratic living demonstrates the fact that a Christian lacks the supply of truth, encouragement and strength that is essential to spiritual sustenance. It is the Word, understood, meditated upon in order to appropriate it, and then followed in day-by-day living that causes fruit to grow for God's honor. Where is the Holy Spirit in all of this? Everywhere, of course! It is He Who enables the Christian to grow in understanding and in his ability to appropriate and apply

God's truth. In the final analysis, all spiritual growth is "brought about by God" (Colossians 3:10).

So, informed Christians will understand and heed what God has to say about these matters. If you are not growing as you should and would like to begin a vital study of the Bible that will lead to fruit-bearing, I suggest that you talk immediately to your pastor and tell him so. If he doesn't know how to help you – and sadly, there are those who don't – then, perhaps, you could begin by studying my book, *What to Do on Thursday.*" That book details a way to understand and use the Bible in day-by-day life. But regardless of how you begin, begin!

15

Renewal of the Image

Unless Calvin somehow equated the restoration of the image of God with the act of regeneration, it is difficult to see how he could speak of regeneration *in part*. The image, it is true, is restored gradually, not all at once. But image restoration and regeneration are not to be equated. The one is an act, the other a work in progress. Regeneration, wholly of God, is the act by which He gives dead sinners spiritual life. This life enables them to believe the Gospel and *subsequently* grow in grace. Restoration of the image of God, lost in the fall, is progressive. Growth implies life (a dead tree doesn't grow); spiritual growth presupposes spiritual life. So, life precedes growth.

The Image Lost

Now, the image of God that was lost in the fall was restored completely in Jesus Christ who, Himself, as the God-Man, is "the image of the invisible God (Colossians 1:15), "the perfect representation of God's very being" (Hebrews 1:3). But it is only being restored gradually in us. Paul speaks of putting on the image as a gradual renewal (Ephesians 4:22–24 and Colossians 3:9–10). In the Colossians passage, the renewal is described as putting on the "new person who is being renewed in such a way as to produce full knowledge that is in keeping with the image of the Creator" (v. 10). In Ephesians, the renewal is said to be a restoration of God's likeness with righteousness and holiness that come from the truth" (v. 24). Together, these two passages indicate that what was lost and, therefore, must be restored was knowledge, righteousness, and holiness. Again, notice, these are renewed through God's Word of truth.

Renewal in Christ

The word for "renewal" in Colossians (and also in Romans 12:2) means "to make new again, to restore to its original condition." It describes the result, but not the cause. The term in Ephesians, however, does refer to the cause. It means "rejuvenated." Making one "youthful again" is an interesting concept. Since the fall, men have become cynical, weary, and worn. There is little incentive to change. But when Jesus Christ gives spiritual life, the "newness" of life that transforms the attitude and thinking of the one He changes so as to give him a new zest additional for change. Before the fall, and the loss of the image of God, as Adam looked out on the freshly created world, and was told to subdue it, he must have thought, "Ah. This pristine creation is mine to work with in order to glorify God and to enjoy it! You can practically hear him saying, 'Just let me at it!'" But in the fall, all of that changed. Work became toil; birth became labor pains. Thorns and weeds began to overgrow not only the fields and the plants, but also Adam's attitude. That newness, which was once so appealing, now was lost. If man was ever to live as God commanded, it would take a renewal of the *attitude* – of the zest – that had been lost. And that is what God did in Christ: He restored not only the ability to gain true knowledge, holiness, and righteousness, but also the desire to pursue them. Like a child, anxious to play with a new toy, the Christian becomes "youthful" (rejuvenated) as Adam was. As a believer learns the truth and transforms it into life and godliness, he becomes more like Christ, Who is in God's image. And the more he becomes like Christ, the more he wants to be like Him in additional respects. That is to say, by his renewed zest for knowledge, righteousness, and holiness, the image of God is gradually restored.

A Process, Not an Act

This process of renewal, once more, envisions gradual rather than instantaneous change: we *are being renewed* after God's image. It is a daily activity in which true believers must be regularly engaged. This renewal means that the regenerate person is gradually able to put off more and more of the "old man" (that is, the person that he was before conversion) and put on more and more of the "new man" (who is the person, like Jesus Christ, that he is becoming). But, once more, the image is *being* restored. It involves a process of learning what God's will is, putting away those things at do not accord with it, and replacing these with the things that please God. The minimalists are right as over against the maximalists when they teach that change is gradual, not instantaneous. Surely, it comes in irregular stages. But what of the elements that are being restored? Are they corrupted by sin? Are they not like the originals? Is this image something less? If so, is there really a restoration? If they are something less, how do they truly reflect God's likeness – especially if the elements of the new image are tainted? These are hard questions that minimalists have not adequately answered.

The maximalists are right as over against the minimalists when they affirm that the effects of regeneration are greater than what the minimalists think. But neither is correct about the degree to which the image may be restored. On the one hand, the maximalists expect to live a "victorious life" through yielding or a second work of grace. On the other hand, the minimalists think that there is very little gain to be had in the restoration of the image in this life, because the renewal is only partial – every step of renewal taken is tainted, polluted, acceptable only because it is forgiven by God's grace. The New Testament, however, presents every element of genuine growth as full, not partial; as good not only partially so. That is not to say complete, but rather that every gain made is a true gain; it is not some sort of defective, corrupted gain. W.G.T. Shedd wrote "The beloved disciple John, also, though he seems to have lived in the spiritual world while he was upon earth...is compelled to say of the Sons of God, 'It doth not yet appear what we shall be.'" It would seem that Shedd was struggling to find the same middle ground that I have been charting in this book. It is possible to live a genuinely spiritual life – the eternal life of leftovers (more than we need) – yet still recognize that we are far from entirely sanctified. That, as he notes, is reserved for eternity. In his seminal work, *The Bible Doctrine of Man*, John Laidlaw expresses the problem this way: "Why is there so little of the new man in the regenerate? Why are the spontaneous products of his heart so corrupt and evil after all? ...Should not the new birth have done much more for me than it has done...? Most Christians will concur in the propriety of putting such questions, though there is no exhaustive answer to them." Even Laidlaw's pen is stopped; he can go no further: "It is plain that some of the questions suggested above can receive no answer."

Let's take a biblical instance: I Peter 1:18, 19. This verse, when translated closely reads,

> "knowing that you weren't set free from the useless behavior patterns that were passed down from your forefathers by the payment of a corruptible ransom... but with Christ's valuable blood...."

Can one really "put off" an old lifestyle? Peter says, "Yes." But he also stated that it is also possible to put on new ways: "Having cleansed yourselves by obedience to the truth you can have brotherly affection without pretense...having been regenerated by...God's living and continuing Word" (I Peter 1:22, 23). Notice the words "without pretense." Do they not indicate that the change is without the supposed corrupting factor that takes the shine off it? Doesn't Peter say that you *can* have brotherly love? Is brotherly love corrupt, marred, tainted and polluted love? Not only is there nothing of the sort in this passage; there is nothing elsewhere to support this belief (cf. Romans 6:17 where Paul speaks of obeying "from the heart" which means genuinely: or as Peter put it, "without pretense").

The contrary view must hold that I Corinthians 6:9–11 refers only to those who had somewhat left behind those practices listed in verses 9 and 10. Because they are somewhat like the AA recoverer who must tell himself every morning as he looks in the mirror, "You are a drunk," the "put off" is not truly a put off after all; it is but only a chaining and suppressing of sin. The Bible, however, seems instead to teach that past sinful ways can be put off and be replaced by new biblical practices so that the person need no longer say "I am a drunk." Back to the apostle Paul who once breathed out threatenings and slaughter against the Lord's disciples (Acts 9:1). When converted, this murderer of God's people truly and completely turned from those ways. I ask you, did Paul have to look into his bronze mirror and say, "I am a murderer. I will have to restrain myself today?"

Without doubt, the Lord Jesus through His Spirit so alters one's individual thoughts and ways that they may become acceptable to God and pass His scrutiny!

16

The Spiritual Life

Christians are "spiritual" persons. In Galatians 6:1, Paul addresses the believers of that church as "you who are spiritual." What does he mean by that? And what effect does the answer have upon the quest for SM? I have said that what every saint needs is not SM, but more of the something that he already has. The "spiritual life," itself, is the "more." And it is "something" that believers already possess! The abundance of this eternal life is what they must be able to enter into more fully. It is, therefore, crucial for us to understand what it is, how it is attained, and what it is able to do for us. Does it satisfy the longing (or should it?). If it does, how can we tap into this life? Where are we failing to do so? What can be done about it? We must try to put those questions to rest.

Spiritual and Carnal Persons

To be a "spiritual" person does not mean that he is one who has exceptional qualities above and beyond that of the ordinary Christian. There are no "classes" of Christians in the Scriptures. All are spiritual. But there are those who do not believe this. Instead, they distinguish Christians who are "spiritual" from those who are "carnal." This distinction comes from a faulty interpretation of I Corinthians 3:1–4:

> Yet, brothers, I wasn't able to speak to you as to spiritual persons, but as to fleshly ones – as babies in Christ. I gave you milk, not food, because you weren't ready for it yet. Indeed, you still aren't ready. You are still fleshly.

When there is jealousy and strife among you, aren't you walking like men without the Spirit? Whenever one says, "I am of Paul," and another "I am of Apollos," aren't you just like such men?

Now, two things ought to be noted from the outset:
1. there is such a thing as a "spiritual" person
2. there is such a thing as a spiritual "walk."

When you see this distinction in the passage, you can understand better what Paul is saying: you are spiritual persons (you have the Holy Spirit), but you don't act like it. Your lifestyle is like that of those who don't have the Spirit. So, since you are walking (living) like fleshly persons (those who do not have the Spirit), I find that I have to talk to you as if you were still fleshly. He does not say that the Corinthians were people without the Spirit – unbelievers. But he says that they were acting like them. In verse 3, when he says, "You are still fleshly," that sentence must be taken in the light of the whole passage, where the emphasis is not upon what they actually are, but what they are acting "like." They were "still fleshly" in their behavior.

The Corinthians, as Paul says in verse 1, were "brothers." That means that they had the Spirit in their lives: "If anybody doesn't have Christ's Spirit, he isn't His" (Romans 8:9). They were members of the household of faith, with Jesus Christ as their elder Brother. To be "in the flesh," as this verse from Romans indicates, is to not have the Spirit dwelling within. Without going into an exposition of Romans chapters 6 through 8 (which I have done in *Winning the War Within*) it is clear from those chapters that walking in the flesh means to walk according to the lifestyle of the unbeliever. It is engaging in this "former manner of life" (the one lived prior to regeneration) or "previous habit patterns" (Ephesians 4:22) that he calls being "in the flesh."

Paul names the problem in biblical terms; they were living like unregenerate persons (v. 3). He does not look for some other underlying psychological difficulty; rather, he rebukes them for their retrogressive, sinful behavior. Then, throughout the rest of the book, he instructs them about how to live according to the Spirit, and encourages them to do so. Since even spiritual persons still sin, they do not always live "in the Spirit." The solution to the problem, then, was for them to stop their unbecoming rivalry and strife and begin to live as spiritual persons should. That is, to live according to the leading of the Spirit.

Walking According to the Spirit

A spiritual person, then, is one who has the Spirit dwelling within (Romans 8:9, 11). When he lives in a spiritual manner – as he should – he conducts his life according to the Spirit's instruction (in His Bible), by the Spirit's urging, and according to Spirit-given ability (cf. Philippians 2:13). In other words, to live spiritually is what Scripture calls walking "*according to* the Spirit" (Romans 8:4, 5). Walking according to the Spirit is to live in the manner I have just described.

Spiritual Life

The spiritual life is the abundant life that Jesus gives to His own. Calvin speaks of the fact that "God renews us and gives us a spiritual life." And elsewhere calls it "a heavenly life" and a "unique life." Packer refers to life according to the Spirit as "supernatural living."

To sum up, spiritual life may be said to be life given through regeneration in which God supplies believers with the Spirit Who

- gives them a new goal (pleasing God; cf. Romans 8:8),
- encourages new thinking (Romans 12:1),
- provides a new kind of peace (Romans 8:6),

- furnishes them with a new ability to serve God through bodies raised out of spiritual death (Romans 8:11),
- grants the ability to overcome evil practices (Romans 8:13),
- and introduces them to this heavenly life as the first fruit of eternal life (Romans 8:23),
- helps in our weaknesses and prayers (Romans 8:25),
- brings us into a filial relationship with the Father (Romans 8:15),
- assures us of our family ties (Romans 8:16)
- and promises an inheritance with Christ when His glory is revealed (Romans 8:17, 18).

That – according to the apostle Paul – is what spiritual life is.

It is also a life of dedicated service to God (Romans 6:13, 16, 19), one in which the Christian considers the present world as something to be "used up," and one that is filled with 'righteousness and peace and joy by the Holy Spirit" (Romans 14:17). Put in another way, see Titus 2:11–14 for a summary of the spiritual life:

> God's saving grace has appeared to all sorts of people, training us to turn down irreligion and worldly desires and to live seriously and righteously and in a godly way in the present age, expectantly awaiting the joyous hope, even the appearance of the glory of our great God and Savior Jesus Christ, Who gave Himself for us to redeem us from all iniquity and to cleanse for Himself a people who are all His own, zealous for fine deeds.

And another summary may be found in I Thessalonians 4:11, 12:

> …eagerly aspire to live a quiet life and mind your own business and to work with your own hands as we have

instructed you, so that you may walk decently before outsiders and won't need to be dependent on anyone.

In essence, these expressions say the same thing, but each adds a dimension. Such a life as this is what the Christian's SM is all about. Obviously, there is much in the Scriptures about the spiritual life. Indeed, much more than I can cover here.

Don't Ruin a Good Start

In a vital passage, Paul speaks about what the Spirit does for the believer. He uses the metaphor of growth, as I have explained. There is a well-known series of verses in Galatians 5. In verses 22 and 23, listing the pieces of fruit that the Spirit produces in the Christian's life, Paul goes on to note that "those who belong to Christ Jesus have crucified the flesh with its passions and desires" (v. 24). And he continues, "If we live by the Spirit; let us also walk by the Spirit" (v. 25). As regeneration occurred by the Spirit's work, so should our life thereafter be motivated and directed by Him. Elsewhere in this same letter, Paul rebukes the Galatians: "Are you really so stupid? Having begun by the Spirit are you going to be completed by the flesh" (Galatians 3:3). That, of course, is the tendency of our embedded habits – to lure us back to the old ways of the flesh by which we lived prior to the coming of the Spirit into our hearts. We are free from their dominion (Galatians 5:24) and need not succumb. We can live in newness of life. We have the Spirit dwelling within to fight against the flesh so that instead of the flesh's works, we might abound in the Spirit's fruit (Galatians 5:17).

Though a heavenly life, of which we have been made partakers, there ought to be nothing about it that is strange to us. To the world? Yes. To us, why? After all, every one of these blessings I have mentioned is clearly spelled out in the Bible – a book that is especially associated with the Spirit Who moved its penmen to write it, and Who illumines us to understand it (cf. I Corinthians

2:10–16). To the extent that we are unfamiliar with this life, and fail to live it, that is our fault. All we need to know about it is in the pages of Scripture. The spiritual life, then, is for spiritual people who are indwelt by the Spirit and who live according to His directions and power. It is that simple – and that profound.

17

So, How About It?

What is the conclusion of the whole matter? Is the quest worthwhile? Is it right? Is it Christian? And, if so, what must you do about it?

The quest for SM is, and is not, Christian depending on what you are seeking and why. The unbeliever's quest – unless he is seeking to find the way of life in Christ – is always illegitimate. That is because it is selfish, it is man-centered, and it focuses on discovering more of those things that displease God. There is, therefore, no sense in which the unbeliever's quest for SM can be legitimate.

The quest for SM among Christians may equally be wrong and displeasing to God. If, by SM, something *else,* something *different,* or something *additional* to his faith is his pot of gold, it is not Christian. If, on the other hand, it is a search for how to better honor God, a search to fill the longing for greater righteousness and holiness, and a search for better ways to become Christ's fruitful servant, then it is preeminently worthwhile and decidedly Christian.

Three Perspectives

The quest for the believer may be considered from three perspectives:

1. What he gets out of it;
2. What he becomes through it;
3. What he does as a result of it.

The first – what the Christian gets out of the quest – is not really his to search for. If he obtains peace and joy through growing knowledge and holiness in the service of Christ, then so be it! Let him be glad and thank God. When other things are right, that wonderful outcome will take care of itself. It needs no searching or seeking. Indeed, it is a by-product; not something to be obtained directly. His happiness will come in the doing" (James 1:25). What *he* gets out of the search should not be the center ring – the bullseye – in the Christian's target. He should not ignore God's goodness in granting such blessings, of course, but neither should he aim at them. While he should revel in them, he should not become satisfied with them. Every blessing should spur him on in the quest for greater love for God and for his fellow man. The spiritual life is one in which he denies and crucifies self daily, and instead of seeking what he wants, one in which he follows Christ more faithfully in an endeavor to do what *He* wants.

The second – what the Christian becomes through it. This is an important matter, perhaps the most important of all. When one fellowships with Christ, as the Spirit molds his thinking and his lifestyle, as he puts off old ways and replaces them with the restored image of Christ, he should become a far different person – one who is becoming more like Christ. One who, thereby, honors Him more fully. Here, the Christian should aim at nothing less than perfection. He knows that he will not reach that goal. But the higher he aims, the more likely is he to make better progress. He must not become discouraged by defeatist talk about not being able to get very far on the path of righteousness. Rather, he should pursue righteousness and holiness with Spirit-led vigor!

The heart of the believer is what determines proper action. It must be cultivated at all costs. Out of it are all the issues of life (Proverbs 4:23). In his quest for SM, the believer must seek to become more and more like His Savior. He must desire to grow into His likeness. He must seek to develop a heart for God – one that is filled with love, and all of the qualities that are associated with love (cf. I Corinthians 13). As he does so, God's image and likeness will be restored more and more fully. In short, a true, God-honoring quest for SM is, fundamentally, a quest for Christ-likeness.

The third – what he does as a result of becoming more like Christ. Here, the entire gamut of Christian behavior and service might come under our purview. But that would require chasing down all that the Bible has to say about life in the Spirit. To pull all of this together, we might simply say that what a person who is seeking and finding *does* is to live a life of gratitude, praising God and ministering to others what He first ministered to him.

Enjoy More of the Something!

You will notice that I have not looked at the quest for SM as something held out in the distance that cannot be reached – or that has not *yet* been reached. In saying that the quest ought to be for more of the something that one already has, I am saying that he *already has* a portion – however large or small – of the something that he seeks. In other words, the proper biblical quest is for greater growth in those spiritual attainments that he has already experienced to some extent. It is truly an adventure into the outer edges of the heavenly life that has been, to a degree, manifested already for the believer in this life. It is a quest in which one may enter into intimate contact with the divine. The concern of the believer, then, is progress in learning, assimilating, appropriating, articulating, and achieving what God desires for him—not something more, but more of the something he has!

Let's look at this in another way. If there are aspects of the Christian life that he does not yet exhibit in his life, the believer must seek these. They are not SM, in the sense that they are different in source, emphasis, or goal. Rather, they are in truth but larger aspects of the spiritual qualities that he already possesses. They may stem from greater knowledge, understanding, and wisdom – but these aspects are not SM; they are more of the same. They will never clash with the true "something" that a Christian already has, but will harmonize with and enlarge it.

It is important to know that in this life, your quest will never end. If it does, you are following the wrong trail. No, your quest will eventually take you across the border from partial to complete enjoyment of the abundant life. Even then, in the eternal, heavenly life when all is finally perfect, without spot or blemish, a new quest will begin. It will not progress from sin to righteousness. You will be altogether righteous in that day. It will take the form of exploring the endless extent of life with God. That too will never end – throughout all eternity. And, even now, when in the present quest you come upon hard times, you always have that future day when you step from this world of sin and misery into glory to look forward to. Then, all of the questions that remain will be answered. There will be nothing but exceeding joy. The superlatives that you have heard will all be realized to the full. You will be in the presence of God, His Son, and the holy angels! Now, that's truly SM! Isn't it?

So, what then, is the upshot of all that we have been studying? In a nutshell, the Christian quest must never be a turning aside from what God has already given him. Rather, it must be a gradual enlarging, deepening, and richer experiencing of the basic beliefs and behaviors that God has ordained for His people's welfare and for the glory of His Name. So, if you have been disillusioned with your Christian experience thus far, count it up to this: you have been yearning for the wrong thing, you have been failing to adequately apply what you have, or you have been attempting to do so in the wrong way. So, what must you do? Examine what the Lord has already done for you and what He has enabled you to do for Him. Discover how these came about. Lay your hand to the task and continue to do those things in the future—to an even fuller and greater extent. If that is your quest, God will lead you to His rainbow, at the end of which you will find a treasure richer than a pot of fine gold!

www.ingramcontent.com/pod-product-compliance
Lightning Source LLC
LaVergne TN
LVHW021408080426
835508LV00020B/2507